Advance Praise for *Endless Referrals* by Bob Burg

"Any entrepreneur or salesperson who doesn't own this book is losing money because of it. Read what Burg has written, internalize it, and then take it to the bank with more money than you'll ever be able to spend. His system works!"

—Wilson L. Harrell, former publisher of
Inc. magazine and contributing editor of
Success magazine.

"Bob Burg's book is a masterpiece! A must for anyone in sales and for anyone wanting to expand their financial and relationship resources."

—Anne Boe, author of
Is Your Net-Working?

"Reading *Endless Referrals* was worth the price of a Harvard MBA. What a great way to have new business beating a path to your door! Free advertising, free pre-sold prospects, free business! A true breakthrough in real world prospecting."

—Tom "Big Al" Schreiter, author of
Big Al Tells All

"Bob takes the art of sales and the art of relating to people and combines them in an incredibly effective roadmap to success and great profits. Buy this book and watch your personal and professional network, and your bank account, grow and grow."

—Pam Lontos, author of
Don't Tell Me It's Impossible
Until After I've Already Done It

"The title of the book says it all. In a clearly written, well organized, easy-to-follow format, Bob Burg shows how anyone can become a master at the art of business networking. Most important, his strategies and techniques are in step with the present and future world of successful selling. Follow Burg's advice and you'll get what the book promises—a steady and growing number of endless referrals."

—Michael LeBoeuf, author of
How to Win Customers and Keep Them for Life
and *Working Smart*

"A quick and powerful read packed full of value. This is great! These are the time-tested, simple things that really work! All of our sales leaders *will* own the book."   —Richard B. Brooke, President and CEO,
Oxyfresh USA, Inc.

"Bob Burg has just taken away all the excuses for not finding clients by showing you step-by-step how to find 'diamonds' in your 'acres.'"

—Danny Cox, author of *Leadership When the*
Heat's On

D0173787

"Great book! Chock-full of helpful information. It's 'must reading' for success-oriented people."
—Kenneth B. Erdman, author of
Network Your Way to Success

"Networking is more than a buzzword for Bob Burg. In his book, he shows how to build and train a networking team that makes prospecting more effective and profitable for everyone."
—Homer Smith, Editor,
Master Salesmanship

"Bob Burg has a knack for connecting with people. In *Endless Referrals* he lays out his techniques in a simple, easy-to-follow format so that you too can develop a knack in connecting with people. This book is well written, well researched, and absolutely practical. I highly recommend it."
—Jim Cathcart, author of
Relationship Selling

"Bob Burg is the greatest teacher of networking in the world."
—John Milton Fogg, author of
The Greatest Networker in the World

"Bob Burg knows what he's talking about, and shares that knowledge clearly and generously with the reader."
—Rabbi Harold Kushner, author of
When Bad Things Happen to Good People

"Bob Burg, in *Endless Referrals*, provides the intellectual structure for what most professionals do—in varying degrees—intuitively. Now, through understanding the process, we can do it even better. To be a *real* pro, read *Endless Referrals*."
—Gerald Coffee, Captain, USN (Ret.),
author of *Beyond Survival*

"I find Bob Burg's networking principles an essential and useful system in an age where soft touch must match high tech."
—Robert Rosenberg, CEO,
Dunkin' Donuts

Endless Referrals

Network Your
Everyday Contacts
Into Sales

Bob Burg

Burg Communications, Inc.
Jupiter, Florida

McGraw-Hill, Inc.

New York   San Francisco   Washington, D.C.   Auckland   Bogotá
Caracas   Lisbon   London   Madrid   Mexico City   Milan
Montreal   New Delhi   San Juan   Singapore
Sydney   Tokyo   Toronto

Library of Congress Cataloging-in-Publication Data

Burg, Bob.
    Endless referrals : network your everyday contacts into sales /
Bob Burg.
        p.   cm.
    Includes index.
    ISBN 0-07-008942-6
    1. Selling.   2. Business—Communication systems.   3. Social
networks.   I. Title.
HF5438.25.B86   1994
658.85—dc20   93-36272
                                                                    CIP

        7 8 9 0   DOC/DOC   9 9 8 7 6 5

ISBN 0-07-008942-6

*The sponsoring editor for this book was Betsy Brown, the editing supervisor was
Joseph Bertuna, and the production supervisor was Donald F. Schmidt. It was
set in Palatino by McGraw-Hill's Professional Book Group composition unit.*

Printed and bound by R. R. Donnelley & Sons Company.

Gender Usage
The author feels very strongly regarding the utilization of gender equal-
ity in his writing. The pronouns *his* and *her*, *he* and *she*, etc., have been
used interchangeably and randomly throughout the text.

To Mom and Dad—Your love, support, and encouragement have kept me going for 35 years. Words will never be able to describe how much I love you and what you mean to me.

To Samantha and Mark, my beautiful niece/goddaughter and handsome nephew—I love you!

Contents

Preface

From the on-the-street salesperson to the doctor, from the entrepreneur to the accountant, endless referrals are the cornerstone of business. Without a business based on endless referrals from present customers and clients to everyday contacts, the fate of anyone's business is a nerve-wracking mystery, dependent upon current economic conditions and buying moods.

But a business based on endless referrals brings peace of mind. Endless referrals is going to sleep at night knowing that the chances are good that you'll have new business waiting for you the next day, and the next, and the next for as long as you desire.

Prospecting is, and always will be, a key to building a business based on endless referrals, but these days, the rules of the game are changing. No longer do standard prospecting techniques work. The average consumer is more knowledgeable, less trusting, and wants to have a "know you, like you, trust you" relationship with his or her salesperson. Nowadays, in order to build that business based on endless referrals, we do it another way. We network!

But, in actuality, that is a confusing word, as misunderstood today as ever. Does it mean handing out business cards? Or aggressively shaking hands with everyone who comes within 3 feet of us? Do we *tell* people we are networking? Where can we do it? Exactly what *is* networking?

In essence, networking is the mutual give and take that results in a winning situation for everyone involved in the transaction.

While the term networking wasn't prominent until the 1980s, it has always existed in some form—as the old boys' network, or the grapevine. Recently, however, networking has become more of an art and science. I realized this as I listened to humorist Roger Masquelier at a National Speakers Association convention. Masquelier was telling a story about networking at a meeting. "Of course," added Roger, "in the old days, we just called it talking." This brought laughter from the audience, and thousands of heads nodding in agreement.

What I realized at that point was that most people actually do believe that networking is merely "talking," as well as indiscriminately handing out business cards. *It isn't.* As misunderstood as networking is, there is a real need for individuals and companies in our modern business scenario to use it effectively.

Why? Because in today's tough business climate, where competition is so incredibly fierce and many markets are already saturated, people are realizing that it's vital to be able to cultivate new business without spending a lot of money doing it.

I like to define *networking* as cultivating mutually beneficial, give-and-take, win-win relationships. For the purpose of this book, the end result may be to develop a large and diverse group of people who will gladly and continually refer a lot of business to us, while we do the same for them.

Throughout this book you will have the opportunity to meet and learn from people who have successfully developed businesses based on referrals by using the techniques described. Do each use all the techniques mentioned? Not at all. Certain people find that some ideas are more applicable than others to their particular profession or method of operation.

This book, therefore, is based not on theoretical pap but on time-tested, proven ideas that have worked for many of us. As you read through, you may at times begin to say to yourself, "That technique wouldn't work for me," or "I could never see myself doing that." If this is the case, you have two choices; one is to not even try it, but the other, more profitable choice is to mold the technique to your particular business style and type of work.

If you follow the techniques with a ready, willing, able, and most of all, open mind, you will soon find yourself cultivating a network of endless referrals.

Bob Burg

Acknowledgments

There are so many people I need to thank that it would take a separate book just to list them. Instead, let me thank several groups of people. One is the National Speakers Association, which has over 3500 of the nicest, most supportive, sharing, and caring people in the world.

Also, my fellow speakers, authors, and salespeople who were so willing to lend their ideas and success stories to this book for the benefit of my readers. Jeff Slutsky, you're a prince.

And those who gave me moral and written support when it was needed (which was always). Dean Shapiro, thank you. Your expert writing skills rescued my readers from many of my overused expressions and amateurish syntax. Lloyd Jones, a wonderful agent and entrepreneur and a true salesperson, and Betsy Brown at McGraw-Hill, your knowledge of the publishing business, encouragement, and professionalism were a guiding light. And you were incredibly great to work with, as well.

I must thank my office staff, who help make my speaking habit possible by keeping me on the road constantly. (Come to think of it, that's probably where they like me best!) Thank you for your loyalty, love, and support.

Of course, I thank my clients, without whom I wouldn't have an audience and the pleasure of involvement in a wonderful, rewarding career such as this.

And you, the reader, for your participation, feedback, and help in making this book a best-seller.

To each and every one of you, I wish you the best of success...AND GREAT NETWORKING!

Bob Burg

1

Networking: What It Is, and What It Does for You!

Og Mandino is an extremely successful man. A renowned speaker and storyteller, he is probably best known as author of the classic best-seller, *The Greatest Salesman in the World*. This book alone has sold well over 30 million copies. Yes, that's 30 *million* copies! And that was just one book. His others also continue to sell extremely well.

In July 1992, Og was the keynote speaker at the annual National Speakers Association convention. For about 45 minutes he talked about the fact that nobody who is truly successful ever does it alone. He talked about his wife, his family, his associates and friends—all the people who had helped him through the rough times and over the hurdles.

But What Does That Have to Do with Networking?

Let's go back to the definition of networking that I gave in the preface. Networking is the cultivating of mutually beneficial, give-and-take, win-win relationships.

Now let's take a look at how Webster's dictionary defines the term *network:* 1. Any arrangement of fabric or parallel wires, threads, etc., crossed at regular intervals by others fastened to them so as to leave open space; netting; mesh. 2. A thing resembling this in some way.

Now, let's leave out the words and thoughts in both definitions that don't apply to us and the purpose of this book and keep in those that do. Oh, and let's substitute the word *people* in the dictionary definition for the words *fabric, parallel wires,* and *threads.* This is what we get:

> *Networking:* An arrangement of people crossed at regular intervals by other people, all of whom are cultivating mutually beneficial, give-and-take, win-win relationships with each other.

The Basic Setup

Let's look at the first part of what we have.

```
  •       •       •       •       •       •       •

  •       •       •       •       •       •       •

  •       •       •       •       •       •       •

  •       •       •      YOU      •       •       •

  •       •       •       •       •       •       •

  •       •       •       •       •       •       •

  •       •       •       •       •       •       •
```

Just as we are all at the center of our own particular universe, we are also at the center of our network. We realize, of course, that all the other people are at the center of *their* network, and that is as it should be.

Each of the people in this network serve as a source of support (referrals, help, information, etc.) for everyone else in that network. Those who know how to use the tremendous strength of a network realize this very important fact:

> We are not dependent *on* each other; nor are we independent *of* each other; we are all interdependent *with* each other.

The true strength really comes through when we realize that all the people in our network are also part of other people's networks that we ourselves don't personally know. And that, indirectly, makes each of those people part of our network too.

Sphere of Influence

Are you familiar with the term *sphere of influence?* Sphere of influence is simply the people you know—people who are somehow, some way a part of your life, directly or even very indirectly.

Your sphere of influence includes everyone from immediate family members to distant relatives: close friends to casual acquaintances, the person who delivers the mail, the plumber, the tailor, the person who cuts your hair—practically anybody who in some way touches your life and whose life you touch.

Have you ever heard of Joe Girard? Based out of a Chevrolet dealership in Detroit, Michigan, he was one of the world's most successful car salespeople. Officially, he was actually the most successful car salesperson in the world for 14 years. That's how long he was listed in the *Guiness Book of World Records* for selling the most cars in the world in a year's time.

In his book, *How to Sell Anything to Anybody,* Girard explains what he calls Girard's Law of 250. Basically, the law states that each of us has a personal sphere of influence of about 250 people. According to Girard, 250 people will attend our wedding and funeral.

Even if his number for a wedding or a funeral seems somewhat high, the 250 figure still works out. For instance, right now, take a pencil and paper and write down everybody you know. Everybody! Add them and you'll see the number will be around 250.

Therefore, figure that every time you meet someone new, that person, even that *average* person, also has about 250 people in his or her sphere of influence. You know that once that person becomes part of your network, another 250 people indirectly become part of your network as well. Cultivate a network of enough new people, and your personal sphere of influence will soar to incredible heights.

This Network Will Increase Our Sales

These days, buyers are different. They are educated, trained, and skeptical. They are backed by consumer protection laws, as it should be. The adage *caveat emptor,* "let the buyer beware," is no longer apropos. Probably the biggest change of all is that buyers are much more relationship-oriented. People want to buy from people they know, like, and trust.

That's where our network comes into play, but in a different way than you might imagine. You may be thinking, "All those people in our network already know us, like us, and trust us. They are our buyers."

No! They are merely the tip of the iceberg. They are a given, and all things being equal, they will buy from us. But if we stop there, we are walking away from a lot of potential business.

Remember, those people are at the center of their own individual networks. They themselves can connect you to at least 250 people. Keep in mind, those 250 have their own 250. Knowing that, and knowing how to work the situation, will result in a ton of new business.

The Golden Rule

> All things being equal, people will do business with, *and refer business to*, those people they know, like, and trust.

This is absolutely the bronze, silver, golden, and even platinum rule of networking. The intent and theme of this entire book is to show you how to get people to know, like, and trust you. Let's take this one more step forward. We also want these people to *want* to see you succeed and *want* to help you find new business. You might say we want these people to be your personal walking ambassadors. That goal isn't particularly difficult to accomplish.

Things Aren't Always Equal

No matter how well people know us, like us, and trust us as a person, we have to be able to come through for them when they give us their business or referrals. If we can't or don't, we'll be in danger of losing not only their direct business but that of their 250-person sphere of influence as well.

For instance, there is a dry cleaning company in my town. The owners and employees are lovely people who I believe *try* to do a good job. However, it just doesn't seem to work. Personally, I can honestly say I know them, like them, and trust them. Trust them, that is, to do practically anything in the world for me—except clean my suits.

Now, the fact that they happen to be dry cleaners doesn't work out particularly well for them. They nearly ruined three of my best suits. They seemed to have trouble following instructions as well. I would tell them that I wanted very light starch on my shirts, but when I'd arrive to pick up my clothes, my shirts would practically be standing at attention waiting for me. It just didn't work out.

After a while, despite my positive personal feelings about these people, I felt I could no longer justify either doing business with them directly or giving them my referrals. If they were anywhere close to their competition, they would, to this day, continue to get my direct business as well as my referral business. But they are not, so they don't. Again, all things being equal, people will do business with, and refer business to, those people they know, like, and trust.

It Isn't Just What or Who You Know

Sure, we've all heard the old axiom, "It isn't what you know, it's who you know!" That saying was usually related to us by a crusty old, macho businessman type, while he knowingly put his arm around us, proud of himself for sharing his eternal wisdom.

Of course, what you know is also important. Let's face it—we must know what we're doing and talking about. We must be able to provide proper guidance to our prospects, customers, and clients. Also, If we can't provide excellent, or at least adequate, service after the sale, we can rest assured we won't be doing business with that person ever again.

We will also lose out on the business of those in their 250-person sphere of influence. Why? Because nothing gets around faster than negative comments. You can also bet those comments will somehow make their way back to the person who used their influence with that person to get you the referral in the first place. That original person will then, of course, have to be removed from your "who you know" list.

Let's face facts, though. In today's world of sales and business, often, in order to get the opportunity to do business with someone in the first place, who you know has become vitally important. But that's not all there is to it.

> It isn't just what you know, and it isn't just who you know. It's actually who you know, who knows you, and what you do for a living.

That is, when that person, or someone that person knows, needs your products, goods, or services. And...

> providing that first person knows you, likes you, and trusts you.

As previously mentioned, our goal is to get as many new people as we possibly can to feel as though they know you, like you, and trust you; to feel that they *want* to see you succeed and actually *want* to help you find new business. Remember, I said that goal isn't particularly difficult to accomplish. It isn't. We do that by networking.

What Networking Isn't

Since we've been discussing the basics of what networking is, let's talk a bit about what it isn't. You see, networking really is the buzz word of the late 1980s and early 1990s. Everyone seems to use the word, and yet many people don't really know what it is and isn't. Generally, the term *networking* is thought to be when a person hands his or her business card to everyone in the world that he or she meets or comes into contact with. The often aggressive shoving of said business card in said contact's face is many times followed by, "Give me a call. I'll cut you a deal," or "If you ever need to buy a whichamahoozee, I'm the one to call."

That is not networking. That is hard-selling, which is the antithesis of networking. We'll talk more about that later. For now I want you to forget about business cards. Well, don't forget about them altogether—they do serve a purpose, albeit a very minor one. In fact, as far as I'm concerned, business cards have three main benefits.

1. The first "benefit" is very tangible, though not to be taken too seriously: you can win a free lunch at a local restaurant by dropping your business card into a fish bowl. Have you ever done that? Won a free lunch? Paid for your business cards, right? Maybe there is such a thing as a free lunch after all.

You can also win a door prize at an association meeting by, again, dropping your business card into a fish bowl. Or you could even win a free book or cassette tape program at a seminar via the same means.

2. This second benefit is a more legitimate one depending upon your profession, although it absolutely is not networking: you can include your business card with your bill payments or with a tip after your meal.

Let's face it, we all have our bills that have to go out each and every month—electric bill, cable TV, water, telephone, mortgage payment, and more. Doesn't it make sense that someone is at the other end receiving the bill payment, opening up the envelope?

Depending upon the type of product or service you represent, if it can potentially fit anybody's needs and you will probably never get to meet that person anyway, you might as well include your business card with your bill payment. You never know what may happen. That person, or someone in their 250-person sphere of influence, may need to buy what you have to sell.

Are you familiar with a man by the name of Tom Hopkins? Tom Hopkins is an internationally known speaker and author of the book, *How to Master the Art of Selling*. Tom got his start as a real estate sales person, and he used to do that very same thing: include his business cards with his bill payments.

One day Tom got a call from a woman who said, "Mr. Hopkins, you don't know me, but my husband and I want to buy a bigger home and would like to talk to you about it." After agreeing that he'd be delighted to do just that, he asked her how she got his name. She replied, "I handle your account at the Gas Company, and I've got about two dozen of your cards in the top drawer of my desk." Apparently, she didn't know who else to call.

Well, I'm sure that the fee Mr. Hopkins earned by helping that woman and her husband acquire a new home more than paid for his business cards for the rest of his life. Now that's probably not going to happen too often. But if it happens even once in your selling career, that's great—you made out on it. The fact is, business cards are so inexpensive that you might as well include them any time you have the chance, again, because you have nothing to lose.

Another thought along the same line: you can also leave your business card with your tip at the end of the meal at a restaurant. You never know. Your waiter or waitress, or someone in his or her 250-person sphere of influence, may need to buy what you have to sell. But when you do that, you need to make sure you leave a big enough tip; otherwise you will be remembered, but it will be for something else.

3. Finally, you can use your business card to get the other person's business card. As far as I'm concerned, this is the one truly legitimate benefit of business cards. But we'll discuss that in greater detail in the next chapter.

Although I make light of business cards, and totally believe they are not worth much more than the paper stock on which they are printed, when used correctly, they do have some genuine value. Obviously, successful salespeople such as Tom Hopkins, Joe Girard, and many others who believe in them are living proof of their use an an effective business tool.

What I'm trying to point out, and even emphasize, is that business cards by themselves are not about to make you, me, or anyone else successful. They are simply an extension of ourselves and what we are doing right.

Now that we've looked at the benefits of business cards and learned how relatively unimportant they are to effective and profitable networking, let's move on.

What we'll discover throughout this book is that networking involves giving to others and helping them succeed in their lives and careers. When accomplished in a pragmatic and organized fashion, we find that we get back tenfold what we put out, both personally and professionally.

Key Points

- Networking is the cultivating of mutually beneficial, give-and-take, win-win relationships.

- We are not dependent *on* each other; nor are we independent *of* each other; we are all interdependent *with* each other.

- Each of us has a personal sphere of influence of about 250 people. And so does every new person we meet.

- All things being equal, people will do business with, *and refer business to,* those people they know, like, and trust.

- It isn't just what you know, and it isn't just who you know. It's actually who you know, who knows you, and *what you do for a living*...providing that first person knows you, likes you, and trusts you.

- Business cards are not a big deal. We need them mainly to get the other person's card.

2

Questions Are the Successful Networker's Most Valuable Ammunition

The famous sales trainer J. Douglas Edwards was among the first, if not *the* first, to utter the phrase, "Questions are the answers." What exactly did he mean by that?

Simply this: In sales, the person who asks the questions controls the conversation. One may ask, "But wouldn't the person doing the talking lead the conversation?"

It would seem that way, wouldn't it? However, when we ask the right questions, we lead the other person exactly in the direction we want them to take. That's why great salespeople aren't pushy. Great salespeople *never* push. They lead!

In fact, Mr. Edwards had another statement that I think is right on the mark.

The only reason for making a statement is to set up another question.

Of course, he was speaking in the context of a sales presentation. Ask questions—the right questions—that will ultimately lead a person to the right decision: buying that salesperson's product or services.

It's Just As Valuable in the Networking Process

The same theory also applies to networking. Recall the basic fact we learned in Chapter 1. Coming on strong—handing your business card to someone and asking for their business or referrals right off the bat— is ineffective.

What we need to do is make an impression at the first meeting that will simply elicit the "know you, like you, trust you" feelings that are necessary for a mutually beneficial, win-win relationship. We do this by asking questions—the right questions, which we'll discuss in a moment.

When and Where Can We Network?

Networking opportunities occur almost every day, practically any-where and any time. We might expect to network at business func-tions, at chamber of commerce functions, on the golf course, in associ-ation meetings, or in organized networking or lead exchange groups.

That's just the beginning, however. Opportunities to meet new net-working contacts and prospects also occur in places and at times we may not realize. Or we may think the situation is not appropriate for networking.

What are some examples? A PTA meeting, the racquetball court, night school class, shopping mall, airplane, casual introduction by a third party—the list goes on and on. How many times have you found yourself in one of these places and you were certain there were some potential business contacts waiting to be discovered? But you also felt that networking would definitely be frowned upon, that it would be considered...well, *tacky* by some...maybe even yourself? Please keep this in mind:

> If you are networking correctly, the other person will never know that you are networking.

The first thing you do is simply introduce yourself to a person you want to meet. Of course, you don't do this in an aggressive, intimidat-ing, turn-off fashion. You don't walk over with your arm stretched out and business card extended. That's important to keep in mind when meeting this person for the first time.

You tell him your name and offer a firm but nonaggressive handshake. He will respond reflexively by telling you his name. Then ask what he does for a living. He'll tell you and ask you the same question. You tell him briefly, but go right back to showing interest in *his* business.

Now ask him for *his* business card. He'll give it to you. *If* he asks for your business card, give it to him. Realize, however, that your card will be thrown out at the person's earliest convenience. More correctly, either it will be thrown out directly, or it will travel through a never-ending dimension of time and space, lost forever in The Rolodex Zone, never to be seen or heard from again. But, as we learned earlier, the main reason for having your business card is not to give it to someone else but *to get the other person's card.*

The next step is very important.

> After the introduction, invest 99.9 percent of the conversation asking that person questions about himself and his business. Do not talk about you and your business.

Why? Because at this point, contacts don't care about you or your business. Let's face facts: your business and my business are probably two of the things in this world that person cares least about. That's just the way it is. He wants to talk about himself and his business. Let him! This is known as being you-oriented. Most people, of course, are I-oriented.

Will this get you off to a good start with your networking prospect? Let me answer that question by asking you a question: Have you ever been in a conversation with someone who let you do practically *all* the talking? If so, did you say to yourself afterward, "Wow! What a fascinating conversationalist!" Sure, we've all done that. Isn't it true that the people we find most interesting are the people who seem most interested in us? You bet!

Warning!

There's a sneaky kind of danger that you need to be aware of at this particular point. Let's pretend the person just asked what you do for a living. When you answer, it just happens to be something that person really needs.

For instance, imagine that you are a stockbroker. You responded not by saying, "I'm a stockbroker," or even "I'm a financial planner," but instead by giving a short benefit statement such as "I help people create and manage wealth."

Now the person looks at you and says, "What a coincidence. My spouse and I were just talking about the fact that we are very weak in that area and need to do something about it. After all, we're working hard, but we have no financial future, nothing put away for the later years. We know we definitely need to talk to a person such as yourself right away."

Let's face it. At this point, everything inside you wants to go *Yesssss!!!!!!*

That, unfortunately, would not be the correct response. As tempting as it might be to try to set up an appointment with that person and his spouse right on the spot, realize that they are just not ready yet. The "know you, like you, trust you" stage has not yet been established. Bombarding that person right now will do just the opposite of what you want to accomplish. Instead, just go right back to asking questions about him and his business.

> The type of questions we need to ask are called open-ended, feel-good questions.

Let's look at both. Most of us who've either read books on sales or taken any kind of sales training are already familiar with open-ended questions. These are simply questions that cannot be answered with a yes or a no, but require a longer response. I first learned about open-ended questions when I was a television news anchor for an ABC affiliate in Oklahoma. Management decided that we should have more live interviews, lasting about 3 minutes, during our newscasts. Now, 3 minutes doesn't seem like a particularly long time to most people. On live television, however, 3 minutes can be an eternity! Especially when it came to some of my guests.

Understandably, they weren't necessarily used to being interviewed on television. Or they might have been brilliant people, but not especially charismatic. For instance, during the oil crisis of the early 1980s, I was interviewing Mr. Johnson from the local bank:

> ME: So, Mr. Johnson, how do you feel the current oil problems will affect the local banks as well as the local residents?
>
> MR. JOHNSON: Uh…it's gonna be tough.
>
> ME: Okay, it's gonna be tough. Can you elaborate on that point?
>
> MR. JOHNSON: It's going to be *really* tough.

I was thinking, "This would be a fantastic time to take a commercial break!" But then I heard the director through the earphones screaming, "Stretch! Stretch! You still have 2 minutes, 30 seconds left!" That was tough! But it taught me that if I was going to survive these 3-minute live interviews, I needed to learn how to ask questions that would get and keep my guests talking.

What I did—and my suggestion to you is to do likewise—was to watch some of the top network television interviewers, people such as Ted Koppel and Barbara Walters. Whether you like them or not, these are people who know how to ask questions that get people talking.

Barbara Walters, of course, asks questions that get people *crying*. That's not good for our purposes. We want to accomplish just the opposite. We want to ask questions that make people feel good about being in a conversation with us. We want to ask questions that make our new networking prospects feel good about us as people, even though we've just met and they hardly know us.

Ten Networking Questions That Work Every Time

I have 10 questions in my personal arsenal. They are absolutely *not* designed to be probing or sales-oriented in any way. You'll notice that they are all friendly and fun to answer and will tell you something about the way that person thinks. You'll never need or have the time to ask all 10 during any one conversation. Still, you should internalize them. Know them well enough that you are able to ask the ones you deem appropriate for the particular conversation and time frame.

Here are the 10 questions.

1. *How did you get your start in the widget business?*
   People like to be the Movie of the Week in someone else's mind. "I worked my way through college, then started in the mail room, then blah, blah, blah, and finally began the fascinating career of selling widgets." Let them share their story with you while you actively listen.

2. *What do you enjoy most about your profession?*
   Again, it's a question that elicits a good, positive feeling. And it should get you the positive response you're seeking. By this time you've got him on a roll.

3. *What separates you and your company from the competition?*
   I call this the *permission-to-brag question*. All our lives we're taught not to brag about ourselves and our accomplishments, yet you've just given this person carte blanche to let it all hang out.

4. *What advice would you give someone just starting in the widget business?*
   This is my *mentor question*. Don't we all like to feel like a mentor—to feel that our answer matters. Give your new networking prospect a chance to feel like a mentor by asking this question.

5. *What one thing would you do with your business if you knew you could not fail?*

   This is a paraphrase of a question from noted theologian and author Dr. Robert Schuller, who asks, "What one thing would you do with your *life* if you knew you could not fail?" We all have a dream, don't we? What is this person's dream? The question gives her a chance to fantasize. She'll appreciate the fact that you cared enough to ask. And you'll notice that people always take a few moments to really ponder before they answer.

6. *What significant changes have you seen take place in your profession through the years?*

   Asking people who are a little bit more mature in years can be perfect because they love answering this question. They've gone through the computer age, the takeover of fax machines, the transition from a time when service really seemed to matter.

7. *What do you see as the coming trends in the widget business?*

   I call this the *speculator question.* Aren't people who are asked to speculate usually important, hot-shot types on television? You are therefore giving them a chance to speculate and share their knowledge with you. You're making them feel good about themselves.

8. *Describe the strangest or funniest incident you've experienced in your business.*

   Give people the opportunity to share their war stories. That's something practically everyone likes to do, isn't it? Don't we all have stories we like to share from when we began in business? Something very embarrassing happened that certainly wasn't funny then but is now. The problem is, most people don't get the chance to share these stories. You, however, are actually volunteering to be that person's audience.

9. *What ways have you found to be the most effective for promoting your business?*

   Again, you are accentuating the positive in this person's mind, while finding out something about the way he thinks. However, if you happen to be in the advertising field, absolutely *do not* ask this question. Why? Because right now, it would be a probing question, and it would be perceived as such by your networking prospect. Eventually you will get to ask that question, but not now.

10. *What one sentence would you like people to use in describing the way you do business?*

Almost always, the person will stop and think really hard before answering this question. What a compliment you've paid him. You've asked a question that, quite possibly, the people who are closest to him have never thought enough to ask.

It's *How* You Ask

You may be wondering if a person will feel as though you are being nosey asking these questions during a first meeting. The answer is no.

Remember, you won't get to ask more than just a few of these questions during your initial conversation anyway. But more importantly, these are questions people enjoy answering. If you ask them the way I have them worded, you won't come off like Mike Wallace conducting an interrogation for *60 Minutes.* We wouldn't want that. These questions are simply meant to feel good and establish an initial rapport.

There are also *extender questions,* which can be utilized effectively when the person's answer needs lengthening. For instance, the words, "Really? Tell me more." The person will usually be only too happy to accommodate you.

Then there is the *echo technique,* taught to me by my friend and fellow speaker, Jeff Slutsky, author of *How to Get Clients.* According to Jeff, you only need to repeat back the last few words of a networking prospect's sentence in order to keep him or her talking. For instance:

> NP (NETWORKING PROSPECT): ...and so we decided to expand."
>
> YOU: "Decided to expand?"
>
> NP: "Yes, we thought the increase in our revenue would justify the cost."
>
> YOU: "Justify the cost?"
>
> NP: "Yes, you see, if the amount of..."

As Jeff warns, however, we must every so often adjust the phrasing of our echo, or eventually the person is going to look at us and say, "What are you anyway—an echo?"

The One Key Question That Separates the Pros from the Amateurs

This next question is key in the process of getting this person to feel as though he knows you, likes you, and trusts you. It must be asked smoothly and sincerely, and only after some initial rapport has been established. The question is this:

"How can I know if someone I'm talking to is a good prospect for you?"

Let's discuss why this question is so powerful. First of all, just by asking the question you have separated yourself from the rest of the pack. It is the first indication that you are someone special. You are probably the only person he has ever met who asked him this question during the first conversation.

During my live seminars where I often address audiences numbering in the thousands, I'll ask for a show of hands from those who have ever been asked that question or even one similar by somebody they have just met. Seldom do more than a few hands go up. Often, none!

You have also just informed that person that you are concerned with *his* welfare and wish to contribute to *his* success. Most people would already be trying to sell their own product or service, but not you. You are wondering out loud how you can help the other guy.

You can be sure that your prospect will have an answer. I was recently talking to a person named Gary, who sells copying machines, and asked him the question. He suggested that the next time I walk by a copying machine in an office, I take a look at its accompanying wastepaper basket. "If that basket is overflowing with tons of crumpled-up pieces of paper," he said, "that's a good sign the copying machine is not working well. That's a good lead for me."

Don't we all have ways of knowing when someone may be a good prospect that the general public does not know? People you meet from now on will be glad to share their knowledge in that area with you. And don't you think they'll appreciate your sincere interest? You bet they will!

Again, that question will be the first indication that you are somebody special and different—a person worthy of doing business with, either directly or by way of referrals. My advice is to learn that question word for word until it becomes part of you and you could ask that question, as the saying goes, "in your sleep."

That question will serve you profitably throughout your life. Loring "Snag" Holmes, an insurance sales professional, found that out right after he attended one of my seminars. About a week after the program, he was introduced to a prospect through a mutual friend.

According to Snag, "When he found out I sell insurance, he immediately became defensive—not the first time I've experienced that response. Before learning these techniques I would've tried to keep selling this person on an appointment. Instead, what I did was focus on him and his business. He seemed to loosen up a little. It turned out that he sold office products. After I asked, 'How can I know if someone I'm talking to is a good prospect for you?' his attitude turned 180 degrees. I should've been asking these questions for the last 30 years."

Alison Oliver, an account executive for a billboard company, was nervous about her brief luncheon appointment with a corporate buyer. He had been tough on the phone, and she was not looking forward to a battle over soup and salad.

"We met for 1 hour and 15 minutes," Alison said, "even though it was obvious he had planned on a much shorter meeting. All I did was talk about his favorite subject—him! Within a week I made the sale, and he personally called my boss to commend me on my selling skills."

These are two incidents that resulted in almost immediate sales, and that isn't even the purpose of this questioning technique. All we are looking to do is establish a positive relationship, which will result in direct business and a lot of referral business *down the road.*

However, these techniques are powerful. Often, they will result in immediate sales. Then we need to maintain the relationship and still work that person's 250-person sphere of influence.

Here's a funny story that truly confirms the power of you-oriented questioning. A good friend of mine in the National Speakers Association, Sydney Biddle Barrows, gained both acclaim and notoriety after her book *Mayflower Madam* hit the best-seller list. It was the true story about the rise and fall of the escort service Sydney had owned. The most successful in New York City.

Understandably, because of the nature of her business, Sydney was not anxious for her friends to know what she did for a living. When people asked her, she would simply ask them something about themselves. According to Sydney, keeping her little secret from her friends was one of the easiest things for her to do.

Countless times, via you-oriented questioning, I've been able to establish excellent contacts on airplane trips. On one occasion in particular, I kept a person talking about himself for the last hour and 45 minutes of the flight. Yes, that took some concentration on my part.

As we landed I said, "If I can ever refer business your way, I definitely will." He replied, "Me too," and I could tell he meant it. Then with an embarrassed smile, he asked, "By the way, what do you do?" Amazing! Just by my focusing on him, he was totally sold on me without even knowing anything about me.

Another time I was sitting next to a syndicated columnist on a flight from Chicago to San Francisco. I asked all about her and her career as a journalist. The result? A feature story on me and my program that ran in all the papers that syndicate her column. This process works!

Back to Your Prospect

So your conversation with your new networking prospect has con-
cluded, and you hardly mentioned yourself and what you do for a living. That's okay, as long as you have *their* card. Later on, we'll look at
how to successfully and profitably follow up with this person.

Key Points

- Networking opportunities occur constantly, anywhere and any time.
- If you are networking correctly, the other person will never know
  that you are networking.
- After the introduction, invest 99.9 percent of the conversation asking that person questions about himself and his business. Do not
  talk about yourself and your business.
- Even if what you do interests the other person right away, turn the
  conversation back to that person and his business.
- Ask several of the 10 open-ended, feel-good questions to find out
  more about your networking prospect. Remember, these questions
  are not intended to be probing in nature, but simply to establish a
  rapport.
- The one key question is, "How can I know if someone I'm talking to
  is a good prospect for you?"

3

How to Work
Any Crowd

Mention the term *networking* to many business owners or salespeople, and images of their local chamber of commerce will immediately spring to mind. Why? Because across North America and throughout the world chambers of commerce have instituted monthly events known as Business before Hours, Business after Hours, Networking Functions, or Card Exchanges.

Regardless of what they're called, the concept is that chamber of commerce members attend these get-togethers with plenty of business cards in tow ready to exchange them with each other. If all goes according to plan, when one of the members eventually needs a particular product or service, he or she will simply have to check their business card file and *voila!* They will know who to go to.

The purpose of this exercise, according to chamber of commerce executives, is, and I quote, "Chamber members doing business with other chamber members." In other words, creating a self-sufficient business environment within the membership.

A Good Thought, But...

It's a great concept! There's only one minor problem—it doesn't work. Why not? Because no matter how loyal people may be to their chamber of commerce, they will most likely only do business with someone for the reason mentioned in Chapter 1. *All things being equal, people will do business with, and refer business to, those people they know, like, and trust.*

Pressing the flesh and handing out an endless number of business cards will not convince people to feel any of these things about you.

And most people simply don't know how to work a chamber of commerce *audience* in such a way as to elicit those feelings. In this scenario, every time you *don't* get somebody's direct business, you also *don't* get the business of her 250-person sphere of influence.

Let us now look at the proven techniques that will allow you to take advantage of a wonderful situation: having tons of good prospects right in front of you for about 2 straight hours.

First, Let's View the Situation

Picture in your mind's eye the typical chamber of commerce card exchange scenario. Let's make believe this one is an after-hours event, usually running from 5 to 7 p.m. The majority of attendees sit at the bar or hang around the hors d'oeuvres table. They have a few drinks, something to eat, talk with each other, flirt with members of the opposite sex, and get absolutely nothing done in the way of business. It's basically a party, and maybe even a darn good party at that, but it isn't networking.

Many people however, rationalize that they are indeed networking. They believe they're doing business because they are at this event after normal business hours. About the most productive thing anybody there is doing is every once in a while meeting somebody they don't know and exchanging business cards. Now, no disrespect meant, but *big deal!*

Oh, occasionally by sheer luck, some business will take place. One person might just happen to need what another is selling, or vice versa. But the chances of that happening are small, and the odds for success are certainly not being played to their full advantage.

The First Thing to Do Is Join

Let me ask you this. If you currently belong to your local chamber of commerce, do you attend these card exchanges? If your answer is yes, have you gotten a ton of business from them? No? Would you like to get a ton of business from them? You can!

The first thing I suggest you do is—if you're not already a member of your local chamber of commerce—join today. For two reasons. One is to do your part in supporting your local business community. The other, and even more importantly, is to have an opportunity to use these techniques during those card exchanges as a real networking and selling tool.

So how do we make these usually social functions become networking and *work for us?* You have to know why you are there—you're not just after these people's business, but that of their 250-person spheres of influence as well. Here are three steps to help you accomplish that goal.

1. *Adjust your attitude.* When I say adjust your attitude, I mean understand that the only reason you are at that particular function is to *work.* That doesn't mean it can't be fun. Networking *is* fun. Establishing mutually beneficial relationships with people is fun. Making more money is fun. But we are there at that card exchange, networking function, or whatever we want to term the occasion, to work.

2. *Work the crowd.* To do this be the "sincere politician"; that is, be sincere, but with an air of confidence about you. Be open, but don't come off like a sharp hustler. Be nice. Have a smile on your face. Very simple, right? Okay. That's a start.

3. *Introduce yourself to someone new.* If possible, introduce yourself to someone who is a center-of-influence type person. These are the people who have a very large and important sphere of influence themselves. Typically, they have been in the community for a long time. People are familiar with them. People know them, like them, and trust them. These centers of influence may or may not be particularly successful in business, but they know a lot of other people whom you want to know.

But How Do We Find Them?

My friend, fellow speaker, and author Rick Hill has a great rule of thumb for locating the function's centers of influence. He notes that people are usually broken up into groups of four, five, or six. According to Rick, each group usually has a dominant person—that one man or woman who seems to control the conversation.

He's right. Next time you're at a chamber of commerce function or social gathering, notice how easy it is to find that one person in every group. When someone in the group makes a point, all heads turn to that person for her response. When our dominant person speaks, everyone hangs on her every word. The group laughs when she laughs. They usually agree with whatever this dominant person says. Remember, that person, while not necessarily financially successful, probably knows a lot of people. Make a point of meeting that person one-on-one.

How do we do that, though, if they are always around other people who are hanging on their every word? Basically, keep your eyes on the few centers of influence as you're walking the perimeter of the room. Eventually, one of them is going to leave his or her present group.

It's the Manner in Which You Introduce Yourself That's Important

Just wait for your opportunity and then walk up and introduce yourself to that person. Perfectly acceptable behavior! Again, that's what you're there for, and so is that person.

If you're sort of embarrassed about introducing yourself cold to somebody, that is understandable. Everyone has those feelings at times, including myself. But realize that if you simply approach that person politely and nonaggressively (without a business card in the person's face and ready to pounce), 99 times out of 100 that person will be quite receptive.

Again, such people know that everybody, including themselves, is there for the purpose of networking, regardless of whether most people know how to go about it successfully. The center of influence is just as anxious to make another contact in you as you are in them.

Now the Process Begins

After you have exchanged names, ask your center-of-influence person what line of business she is in. She'll tell you and ask you the same. That's a start. Respond *briefly* with your benefit statement, then quickly move on to the next step. Remember…

> After the introduction, invest 99.9 percent of the conversation asking that person questions about herself and *her* business. Do not talk about you and your business.

After reading the last chapter, you know why. Your networking prospects don't yet care about you and your business. They want to talk about themselves and their business. Let them. Now is the time to ask several of the 10 questions we discussed in Chapter 2. If you don't remember what they are, go back and review them before you attend your next business function. And *memorize* them: they are the tools you'll need here.

The Question That Separates the Pros from the Amateurs

Remember the most important question in Chapter 2? Now's the time to ask it.

> "How can I know if someone I'm talking to is a good prospect for you?"

We discussed previously why this question is so important. I guarantee you will be the *only* one there asking that question (unless somebody else at that function has already taken my course or read this book). In any case, that person will be more than happy to tell you what to look for in a prospective customer. They will be impressed with you and your concern for them. Believe me, this technique works!

At this point you might be asking yourself, "If everybody knows these techniques, doesn't that take away my advantage?" Here's my answer. These techniques are intended to result in a mutually beneficial, win-win situation for everyone involved in the process. That being the case, doesn't it figure that the more people who know these techniques, the better for everyone involved?

The main thing is to learn this important networking principle, internalize it, and apply it consistently. Those who do will likely attain great success. But the fact is, most people won't. I sincerely hope you are one of the small percentage who will.

Now's the time to *ask for your prospect's business card*. Again, if she asks for yours, give it to her, but realize that the key is to get *her* card. We'll see why in great detail in the next chapter.

Remember Her Name

Later on, *pop back by and call your networking prospect by name*. Let's say it's half an hour later. You're standing at the hors d'oeuvres table by a recently met center of influence. You very pleasantly say, "Hi, Ms. Gregory. Are you enjoying yourself?"

That's really going to impress her, especially because by this time she has more than likely forgotten your name. Well, I guarantee you that at that point she will take notice of your name.

Remembering peoples' names and faces is a very valuable skill, and one that virtually anyone can learn. We'll cover that important networking skill in detail later on.

Matchmaker, Matchmaker, Make Me a Match

If you have the opportunity, *introduce people you have met to others.* Preferably, people who can be of mutual benefit to one another. You should be able to make several good contacts at these meetings. So introduce these people to each other.

I call this "creative matchmaking." Position *yourself* as a center of influence—the one who knows the movers and shakers. People will respond to that, and you'll soon become what you project.

Give each person a nice introduction and explain what the other does. Suggest ways they can look for leads for each other. Remember the critically important step we talked about earlier: asking that person how you can know if a person you're talking to can be a good prospect for them?

Tell Jerry how to know what would be a good lead for Mary, and vice versa. Wow! Will they be impressed! They're going to be reminded that you cared enough about them to really listen and remember. It will show sincere interest on your part, and that will make those people more interested in helping you.

All this time you're just beginning to give them a hint of the fact that you are an ace, someone to do business with or refer to others.

Decide in Advance Who Your Networking Prospects Are

Incidentally, another way you can ensure meeting people with whom you can have mutually beneficial networking relationships is to introduce yourself to people involved in professions complementary to yours. For instance, a mortgage broker should try and meet Realtors® who can refer plenty of business their way. Why? Because Realtors are always working with people who need to borrow money.

How will you know that a person is a Realtor before introducing yourself? Be creative. You can check your chamber of commerce directory beforehand and find out who does what. Ask others who might know who the most influential Realtors happen to be.

Keep Your Eyes and Ears Open

Another method is name tags. You may have spotted a real estate company name on someone's name tag as you passed by each other. Or you might have overheard a part of a conversation indicating that the person is a Realtor. You'll find a way to know if you want to know badly enough.

If you create computer software programs, then meeting a person who sells computer hardware would certainly be a positive step in the right networking direction, wouldn't it? A sign shop owner should try to meet those who either buy signs or, more importantly, are in a position to talk to many other people who buy signs. In any case, regardless of how you meet your best contacts, our next step will be to cultivate them successfully.

Now the business function has ended. Hopefully, you've met about five or six good contacts. Even one or two would not be bad—that's all you need. One or two good contacts are much better than just handing out a bunch of business cards to people with whom you will never end up doing business. That's what everyone else was doing. You've taken a different, more personal approach. The scenario is now set for the follow-up.

In the next chapter, we'll look at some methods of profitable follow-up. Simple in their application, they are designed to ensure that when the time comes that your prospect needs your products, goods, or services (or knows someone else who does), you will be the only one who could possibly be in that person's mind.

Key Points

- Chamber of commerce functions (as well as other business and social events) are excellent sources of networking if used correctly. Otherwise they are practically worthless.

- There are seven proven techniques that will ensure your success at business functions:

  1. Adjust your attitude. Realize that the purpose of attending this function is to work and build your network.
  2. Work the crowd. Be pleasant and approachable.
  3. Introduce yourself to someone new. If possible, have that person be a center-of-influence person. (You can also predetermine with whom you wish to network based on complementary professions.)
  4. After the introduction, invest 99.9 percent of the conversation asking that person questions about herself and her business. Do not talk about yourself and your business.
  5. Ask for *your networking prospect's* business card.
  6. Later on, pop back by and call that person by name.
  7. Introduce people you have met to others.

4

Profitable Follow-Up Techniques

Thus far, we've done well in finding and meeting our networking prospects. Maybe we've done this by way of chance meetings or non-business occasions, or possibly during an organized chamber of commerce function. We've made a great, positive impression on those we've met. Now comes the follow-up. By systematically and consistently implementing the following techniques we will separate ourselves, the successful networkers, from the "wanna-bes."

I know. You're thinking to yourself that follow-up is a royal pain. It can be, but only if you do a lot of unnecessary, time-consuming tasks that don't get results. What I want to do is show you some techniques that, once internalized as good habits, will not seem like a hardship. But they will help you build a powerful network, resulting in a lot of referral business.

Hit Them Right Away

First off, *send a personalized thank-you note.* Sure, we've all been taught that. Basic Sales Training 101, wasn't it? However, very few people actually do this, not realizing they are missing out on an important step. People who send notes get remembered for two reasons.

1. They stand out from the competition, since they are one of the few.

2. The recipient will actually see who it is sending them that note.

More on that in a moment.

In most communities you can mail a letter before midnight and it will arrive at its intended location the very next day—assuming, of course, that the destination is local. A letter that shows up at the person's desk or home the day after you meet is a nice touch.

This note should be a nonpushy, simple, brief note, written in blue ink (research indicates blue ink is more effective both in business and personally). It should say something like, "Hi Dave (or Mary, or even Mr. or Ms., depending upon the particular situation), Thank you. It was a pleasure meeting you. If I can ever refer business your way, I certainly will."

The Impression That's Being Made

Let's look at what you've done. First of all, you have again shown that you have a lot of class and that you are conscientious. You've shown that you are a person worthy of doing business with directly or having business referred to.

What you didn't do was come on strong and try to do a hard sell. You simply thanked him or her just for the meeting (we all like to be thanked, don't we?). You also let that person know once again that you have *their* best interests in mind, with the promise to make an effort to send business their way.

Sure, you could add something about keeping you in mind if they, or someone they know, ever needs your products or services. I'm going to strongly suggest, however, that you don't do that. They understand why you sent them the note and are already impressed with you. Sometimes the more we understate our case, the more dramatic an impact we'll make. Besides, you're going to give them plenty of opportunities to be thinking of you in the very near future.

Let me share with you what I do, regarding the type of stationery for the note you send. I send mine on an individually designed postcard that measures $3^{1}/_{2}$ by 8 inches. In the top right-hand corner is my company name and logo. Beneath that is my picture. Just beneath the picture is my name. Below that is my company address and telephone number. All of this is on the right-hand side of the postcard, leaving plenty of room for writing the note.

Picture This

The picture is very important. You want them to *know* who sent that note, and without your picture they might not. People today meet many other people during the course of a day. As impressed as they were with you during the meeting, as the saying goes, "out of sight, out of mind." What we're doing is giving them a quick reminder right off the bat.

Although this is only the first step toward having them see your face whenever they, or someone they know, need your products or services, it is still an important one. For maximum effectiveness you must put your picture on an individually designed postcard.

Ask your local printer to typeset and print these for you. The expense is minimal; the payback is well worth it. I highly recommend that you get this type of postcard.

First Class All the Way

Now, back to the sending of this note. Although it can be sent as a postcard, I suggest instead enclosing it in a regular number 10 envelope. Address the envelope by hand (again, in blue ink) as opposed to typing it. Do not put a mailing label on it, or on anything else you ever send to this person. I'm not a big believer in using mailing labels because I want the person receiving the information to *know* I really care. Hand-stamp the envelope (as opposed to using a postage meter). An even nicer touch is to use a large, commemorative stamp.

In other words, personalize it. Make it special in your networking prospect's mind's eye. You want this envelope to be opened and the message actually read. If it looks like junk mail, it could be thrown out before ever having been opened. A hand-addressed, hand-stamped envelope will grab people's attention more effectively than one with an impersonal mailing label and postage meter.

Since we've done it the right way, let's take a look at our networking prospect's probable response. He sees the envelope on his desk the next morning. Because it appears to be a personal letter, he opens it. Chances are he still won't, at this point, even associate you with the company name on the envelope. Remember, out of sight...! Now, as your networking prospect pulls out your postcard note and sees your picture, he remembers the good feelings associated with you. You are the one who asked all those questions. You made him feel important. You asked how you could help him, and even introduced him to others.

However, your prospect now thinks, here comes the solicitation. "If I can ever sell you, or someone you know, a whichamahoozee, let me know." But you didn't do that, right? Far from it!

All you did was say thank you for the meeting and let him know you'll try to refer business to him. He will certainly appreciate you for thinking that highly of him, and will remember the effort.

Make the Time

Some people might be thinking, "I'm too busy. I don't have time to write a thank-you note to every new networking prospect I meet." My answer to them is, "Yes, you do!"

The pros, the champions, the ones who are determined to succeed (and you're one of them), do the little things right, consistently. That includes writing and sending the notes.

I say that because through the years I've noticed that successful people share similar traits. One is that they are avid note-writers. They write thank-you notes all the time. It's a known fact that George Bush did this from early on in his career; he networked his way up to the position of chief executive of the United States of America.

There are those who will put the cart before the horse and say it's because these people are successful that now they have the time to write those notes. But we all *know* that's not true. They were doing the little things right, such as writing notes, *before* they were successful. Now it's simply something called "habit."

It's the same in practically every profession. Show me an avid note-writer and 9 times out of 10 I'll show you a success. It's ironic that one trait, such as writing notes, seems to separate those who are successful from those who are not.

From Negotiating to Horse Races

One person who's been a big influence on me is Dr. Jim Hennig. He is an authority on the art of win-win negotiating. Dr. Hennig points out that in negotiating, "It's often the little differences that make the big differences." He goes on: "Doing the little things right can often be the difference between the successful and the unsuccessful negotiation."

That's so true, isn't it? It's true of just about everything else in life. After all, don't they say, "Baseball is a game of...inches." In boxing a split decision is often the difference between the champion and the person who's name we forget 2 weeks later. Maybe even the next day. An average of just a few strokes makes the difference between the top PGA or LPGA money winners and those that barely survive the tour.

My brother Rich is a big horse-racing buff. Recently he gave me an excellent analogy of how little things mean a lot. Typically, in a $200,000 purse, the horse that finishes first brings in $120,000 for its owner. The second horse, who may have lost by just a nose in a photo finish, brings in $40,000 for its owner. The third horse, who lost by just a neck, brings in about $12,000. And the fifth horse, who lost by just a length, one-fifth of a second, brings in the *whopping* sum of $3,000 for its owner!

In that case, couldn't we say that one-fifth of a second was what made the difference of $117,000 between the owners of the first horse and the fifth horse? As Dr. Hennig says, little differences make the big differences.

Back to our thank-you notes. Those of us who are committed to realizing the benefits of effective networking write them even when we don't want to. Let me share with you a shortcut that will make the process a bit easier.

During some downtime, simply take 25 or 30 of your personalized postcards. Leave room at the top for the salutation, and write, "Thank you. It was a pleasure meeting you. If I can ever refer business your way, I certainly will." And sign your name.

I think you know what I'm getting at. Put an elastic band around the postcards, and place them neatly in a shoe box inside the trunk of your car, along with an equal number of already hand-stamped envelopes.

From now on, whenever you meet new networking prospects, simply go to your car, write their name at the top of the note, hand-write their name and address on the envelope (that's why you took their business card), and drop it in the nearest mailbox. Sure, it's still a little bit of extra work, but as speaker and best-selling author Zig Ziglar says, "You don't pay the price for success, you enjoy the benefits of success."

Keep in mind that sending the note is simply a way of establishing yourself and your credibility with this person. It usually will not get immediate results. However, that's not to say, never.

As a speaker and member of the National Speakers Association, I know that other speakers, because of the diversity of topics, are often a tremendous source of referral business. On one particular occasion I was in the audience while a fellow speaker I had not yet met gave a wonderful presentation. We talked briefly afterward and I sent him a note. He, also being an active networker, responded with a note of his own. He also gave me a referral, which turned into a booking.

Naturally, I immediately wrote him a note to thank him for the referral and to assure him that the meeting planner to whom he referred me would receive the highest professional courtesy and so forth.

He then wrote me back a very nice note thanking me for the thank-you note for the referral. In his note he wrote, "It's obvious, Bob, that you are a true professional, and I'm happy to give you referrals."

Remember, at that point he had never actually seen or heard me speak. Since then we've become friends, and I've had the opportunity to refer him to many meeting planners and vice versa. A true win-win.

So don't forget, a simple note or two or three can do wonders when it comes to networking. Don't you enjoy receiving thank-you notes? I do. And I remember those who send them.

Keep Them in Your Thoughts

Be sure to send any articles, newspaper or magazine clippings, or other pieces of information which relate to your networking prospects or their business. If you hear of something that may be helpful to them, send it on your personalized postcard.

For example, a networking prospect sells temporary services to businesses. You hear a rumor that a large company is about to open in a certain building. That would make an excellent and much appreciated informational note, wouldn't it? You could simply call the person, but I would drop a note as well. Dropping that note is so effective and will work to your advantage. A sample might be, "Mary, a quick note to let you know Amalgamated International is about to open in XYZ building. Thought it would be a good prospective lead. Good luck." Then sign your name. Now can't you see how the person on the receiving end of that note would appreciate your unselfish gesture?

Sending newspaper or magazine articles affecting our networking prospects is a very valuable idea. I know, it's another point we all learned in Basic Sales 101, but how many people actually do it consistently?

One challenge people might create is to limit their horizons. You might be thinking, "Well how often does someone in my network actually get his name or picture in the newspaper? Maybe the special Monday business section if they got promoted or something, but how often does that happen?"

Here's a suggestion: as you look through the newspaper, *scour* it to see what bits and pieces of news or information somehow, in some way, affect those in your network. If something you read has anything to do with them, their profession, personal interests, hobbies, whatever, send it along with a short note.

Let me sight a firsthand example. When I was in local sales, I did my networking locally, of course. One prospect in particular was definitely a center-of-influence person whose business and referrals I very much wanted. He was also a direct prospect, as he owned and ran a local franchise business.

One morning in the newspaper, I saw a rather uncomplimentary article about the headquarters of that franchise. This can be a rather touchy situation because we don't want to send our people bad news. Nonetheless, I cut the article out of the paper and wrote a note on my postcard, saying, "Although I don't agree with the article, I thought it would still be of interest." I enclosed the article and note in an envelope and sent it.

He called the very next day to thank me for my consideration. He hadn't seen the article and was glad I cared enough to send it. In fact, he planned to write a rebuttal letter to the editor as a result, which he did. Let me ask you, did I get his business that day? No. But I did 2 months later when he was ready.

In other words, when he needed the products or services that I handled, I was the only one who came naturally to his mind. The founder of the National Speakers Association, Cavett Robert, said it best: "People don't care how much you know until they know how much you care—about them and their problems."

After knowing how much I cared, he was more than willing to find out how much I knew. Over time, I also received numerous referrals from him, and totally believe I would to this day if I were still in that or any other type of local business.

Small Investment—Big Payback

Next, *send your networking prospects a notepad every month or so to keep you on their mind.* This notepad should contain your company name, logo, and your picture, and as on the postcard, your name should be directly beneath the picture.

Your address and telephone number should also be included. Make sure to keep all the information about you on the top quarter of the page. That way they will have plenty of room to write their notes. Otherwise, of course, they'll throw it out.

Practically everyone uses scratch pads or notepads, and when people constantly see your picture, you become familiar to them. Your networking prospects are going to have your face right in front of them a lot of the time. Your visibility and credibility will increase in their mind.

You see, what you really want is for your networking prospects to think of you and *only* you whenever anything is brought up concerning your business. If you're a Realtor, you want them thinking of you whenever they think of buying or selling a home. And more importantly, whenever they hear anybody else talk about buying or selling a home. In fact, whenever they think "home," you want them to think of you. If you're an insurance agent, you want them to think of you whenever "insurance" comes up in a conversation. If you're a copy machine salesperson, you want them to think of you whenever "copy machine" comes up, and so on.

One time, my director of marketing called a prospect on the other side of the country, because she knew it was planning time for their annual convention. The moment my name was mentioned, the meeting planner said, "Oh yes, I have his notepad right here on my desk.

How's he doing?" Please keep in mind, at that time I had never personally spoken to that meeting planner. Nevertheless, she felt she knew me, by virtue of seeing my picture every single working day.

The result was that we got the booking. I'm positive the decision to have me present a program at their convention was *not* based solely on the notepad. But I *am* certain that it opened the door, kept me in the ball game, and kept the benefits of my program on that person's mind.

The Opposite Is Also True

Ethel is a Realtor and a member of a large office. She has lived in her community all of her life and is well liked and respected. One day she ran into a woman with whom she had been friends for years. The woman said excitedly, "Ethel, you're going to be very happy to know I just listed my home for sale with one of the salespeople in your office."

Ethel, for reasons easy to understand, was not exactly delighted by that news. She nicely, but disappointedly, asked, "But we've known each other for years. Why didn't you list it with me?" The woman, now realizing the situation replied, "Ethel, I'm so sorry. I just didn't think of you at the time."

What that shows is that people generally don't care about our success as much as we do. That isn't surprising. People are concerned with their own success. If we are not somehow in front of them at the very time of a buying decision (whether they are buying directly, or in a position to refer business), there's a chance they may not think of us until it's too late.

Another case in point concerns a person in my town who tried to sell me a cellular phone for two years. Every so often I'd get a call from him, and he'd ask me if I was ready to buy. I'd always decline. I mean, I really didn't feel I needed one and wasn't in any particular hurry.

As far as one day possibly doing business with him, that wasn't a problem. He certainly fit into the "knowing, liking, and trusting" category. I always figured when I was ready to invest in a cellular phone, he'd get a call.

But something happened to change that. My parents live just 5 miles from me, and every couple of weeks they travel 2 hours to Miami to visit their two grandchildren. There's one stretch on the Florida turnpike that is fairly deserted. I was always concerned about their car breaking down in the middle of nowhere, with them not being able to contact anyone for help.

We have a rule in our family. Whenever any of us takes a trip of any substance, whether by car or plane, we always call to say we arrived safely. On this particular occasion, however, they didn't call until well after the time they should have. When my dad finally called, he told me what had happened. Their car had broken down in that very stretch I mentioned earlier.

Fortunately, a tow truck happened to be in the area and everything turned out fine. (Thank goodness that kind of luck is typical with my dad.) Nonetheless, the incident was enough to motivate me or, more correctly, panic me into purchasing a cellular phone for them!

I immediately reached for the Yellow Pages and began looking for car phone companies to call. Later that day, a salesperson returned my call. We immediately set up an appointment. We met, I bought a car phone, and gave it to my parents.

The question I ask you now is, what happened to the local cellular phone guy I knew? I'll tell you what happened. I don't know! Actually, I hadn't even thought about him. I was so emotionally wrapped up in the situation with my parents that I didn't even consider calling him. I ended up purchasing the phone from another salesperson, a relative stranger.

However, what if every other month or so I had received a notepad from this guy with his name and picture on it. Wouldn't he, especially in time of panic, when I wasn't thinking logically, have been the only person I would have thought of? Absolutely. I would have reached for his notepad just as easily as I did for the Yellow Pages!

We've got to keep ourselves in front of our networking prospects constantly. Of course, we must accomplish this in a very nonpushy, nonthreatening, almost subliminal manner. The goal is to be the only one they think of when it comes time for them, or anyone in their sphere of influence, to need or want our products, goods, or services.

Newsletters, pens, magnets, and other promotional items are fine. They can never hurt. The problem is that either their shelf life isn't long, as in the case of the newsletter, or they don't have your picture on them and can't always be seen by your networking prospect anyway. A pen will run out of ink and be thrown away and there goes your name and phone number. The scratch pad will be kept and used.

This Sums It Up

In a nutshell, here's why the scratch pad, always on their desk or near their telephone, with your picture on it, is so important. You want them, when they *hear* your name, to know your face and what you do for a living. You want them to *see* your picture and make the connection between your name and what you do for a living. And when they, or someone they know, want or need what you have to offer, you want them to immediately *think* of your name and know your face.

Thanks for the Referral

When you receive a referral (and after implementing these techniques you'll receive plenty), be sure and follow up every time, immediately, with a handwritten, personalized note of thanks. I suggest using the personalized-postcard format we discussed earlier. Again, enclose it in a number 10 envelope for that extra touch.

The note should read something along these lines: "Dear Mary, thank you so much for your nice referral of Bob Jones. You can be assured that anyone you refer to me will be treated with the utmost caring and professionalism."

Now isn't that effective? Short, sweet, professional, and to the point. It says it all. Not to mention that it will surely reaffirm the referrer's feeling that you were the right person for that referral.

Of course, depending upon the situation you can alter the wording of the note or even the type of thank you. I've sent flowers to people who gave me really big referrals. It's certainly worth the investment, as well as a nice way of saying thank you to someone you genuinely like and to whom you feel grateful.

However you thank them, do it in such a way that separates you from the rest. Constantly show that person why *you* should be the only person in your particular line of work receiving the referrals of his or her 250-person sphere of influence.

Key Points

- Follow up on networking prospects in these ways:
  1. *Send a personalized thank-you note* on a 3½-by-8-inch personalized postcard which includes your picture. The note should be written in blue ink, enclosed in a number 10 envelope, and hand-stamped. Make the time to consistently write and send these notes.
  2. *Send any articles, newspaper or magazine clippings, or other pieces of information which relate to your networking prospects or their business.* If you hear something which may be helpful to them, send it on your postcard.
  3. *Send your networking prospects a notepad regularly to keep you on their mind.* Include your company name, logo, picture, and contact information.
  4. Send thank-you notes after receiving referrals.

5
Training the People Who Network for You

Thus far we've learned a method for effectively meeting people and winning them over in a very nonaggressive, nonthreatening way—everything from the initial introduction to your networking prospects through genuinely caring follow-up.

You may have even already matched some good people with other good people and had a hand in the success of those you've chosen to include in your network. It's probably safe to say that these people feel good about you. They know you, like you, and trust you. They want to see you succeed, and they want to help you find new business.

However, there is still a challenge: although these people might *want* to help you find new business, they might not know how. Even though you may be in a profession in which your prospects seem obvious, and people might be totally familiar with what you do, it doesn't matter. For them to know how to network for you may be more difficult than you realize.

Help Them Help You

What you've got to do is make it easy for them. Train the people who want to network for you. Sometimes, things we take for granted are confusing to someone else. Have you ever had a good acquaintance or a close friend whose means of making a living was not known to you?

A friend of mine named Tom is vice president of an engineering firm. When asked what he does for a living, he replies, "I'm an engineer." What does that tell me? What does that tell anyone? Nothing. I'd like to refer business to him when and if the opportunity arises, and I've asked him numerous times to explain, in layperson's terms, just what it is he does and who his prospects are. I still don't understand. He hasn't developed a simplified method of explaining it.

Another friend is a computer consultant. A computer consultant? What is that? It could mean anything, couldn't it? It reminds me of the movie *Father of the Bride*, starring Steve Martin. His soon-to-be son-in-law described himself as an international computer consultant; then he quickly added that he realized it sounded as though he were unemployed everytime he said that.

Even the more tangible types of professions can also be trouble for those who are not versed in that particular field. So let's use a technique usually involved in a one-on-one sales presentation to get our point across.

Features Versus Benefits

What's the difference between a feature and a benefit? A feature is what something *is*, whereas a benefit is what something *does*, or can be something that solves a problem. The difference between features and benefits is often stressed in sales training classes for use during a sales presentation. That's because it is important for sales professionals to realize that people buy a product or service not for its features but for the benefits they will realize by taking ownership.

Keep in mind that benefits often encompass opposite ends of the spectrum. In other words, the benefits include the fulfillment of a desire and/or the solution to a problem.

When I was in direct sales we used to use the analogy of the elderly woman from the cold Northeast. She visited an appliance store in the middle of a freezing winter in order to purchase a heater. The salesperson began rattling off all of the heater's wonderful features, and he was undoubtedly a glib presenter.

He expertly informed the woman what type of material the heater was made of, the way it was crafted, and even the BTU output. He described the engineering and research that went into it, the bells and whistles. He even told her about where it was made and how long the manufacturer had been in business. After patiently listening to this salesperson's eloquent description of the impressive list of features, the woman asked meekly, "But will it keep an old lady warm at night?" *That's* the difference between features and benefits.

A friend of mine and fellow speaker, Frank Maguire, is one of the founders of Federal Express. According to Frank, "We decided early on that we were not in the `delivery' business...but in the business of `peace of mind.' Our clients' biggest fear was late delivery."

Late delivery could ruin their business or, at the very least, ruin a good account. It was their biggest perceived problem, or pain. Frank knew his clients needed to feel assured that, regardless of the situation, their package would "absolutely, positively" be there when it was supposed to be (overnight!).

Life insurance is a feature. Protection and security are the benefits one derives from owning a life insurance policy. For a life insurance sales professional to say, "I sell life insurance" is to merely point out a feature. On the other hand, "I show people how to plan for a sound financial future while protecting themselves and their loved ones for the present, through insurance" is the benefit to the prospective client. In this case, it both satisfies a want (a sound financial future) and solves a problem (protecting the insured's loved ones).

"I sell real estate" is a feature. "I help people successfully market their home and purchase their perfect dream home" is the benefit one will derive by working with that salesperson.

"I am a dentist" is a feature. "I provide healthy teeth and smiles, with no pain" (as opposed to, "I stick metal objects into people's teeth") is the benefit to the prospective patient. And the referrer will easily understand that.

Remember, as we network we have to realize that it isn't only the person to whom we are speaking whose business we are after: more important is his or her 250-person sphere of influence. Stating the benefits of what we do provides our networking prospect with a much clearer picture of who would be a good prospect for us.

Actually Tell Them *How* to Know

There's another step to this as well. Remember the one key question you asked this person during your first conversation: "How can I know if someone I'm talking to is a good prospect for you?" Well, after your win-win rapport is established with that person, you can also let him or her know, in plain and simple language, how to recognize if someone would be a good prospect for you.

For instance, there was the earlier example I cited of Gary, the copying machine salesperson. He made reference to the fact that when walking by a copying machine you might notice a lot of crumpled-up pieces of paper overflowing from a wastepaper basket. According to Gary, that's an indication that particular copying machine has not been working well lately. Its owner might need a new one, and you could be giving an excellent lead.

You can also give others the same type of coaching. If you are a printer, you might suggest that a person just starting a new business may be a good prospect for you. If you are a solar energy equipment salesperson, then suggesting that your fellow networkers keep their eyes and ears open for people complaining about high energy costs would also serve you well. Even though *you* know what it is you need, the chances are, the other person doesn't. Help them to help you.

Keep in mind that no matter how good a rapport is established during your initial conversation with networking prospects, it's only after you have earned their loyalty that you can legitimately expect your benefit statement and prospecting tip to carry any weight with them. That's okay. We're assuming that at present, they are quite grateful to have you in *their* network, and are only too happy to be your walking ambassador.

Your Personal Benefit Statement

We've covered possible benefit statements for several professions. Later in this chapter, I'll list a few more suggestions. Unfortunately, there is not enough room to write out a different benefit statement for every single profession, but you will at least get a sampling of how it's done.

So you need to come up with your own. Let me give you some guidelines first. Your benefit statement should be a short, succinct, descriptive sentence no more than 7 seconds in length. It should describe what you do and how it will benefit the person using your services.

What I suggest is that you develop this benefit statement and practice it on people you know. A family member or close friend is ideal, as well as a trusted associate with whom you work. Get their critique and ask them to be totally honest. Don't worry about perfection. Don't worry about getting your feelings hurt. Your first try isn't etched in stone. You'll keep improving on it as time goes on.

In my case, when I first began teaching networking techniques, my benefit statement was, "I show people how to network for profit." It was a decent benefit statement because it had a desired benefit to the person attending my seminar, namely, profit.

It was decent, but not spectacular. I kept working on it and asked myself the benefit my prospects would get out of my program. Benefits that were tangible, that they could relate to, and that would tell them *how* they were going to achieve all that profit.

Well, I knew my prospects fit into two main categories. The first category was direct salespeople depending on referrals in order to accelerate their business. The second was professionals such as chiropractors, dentists, lawyers, and accountants—people whose business greatly depended on referrals, but who definitely do *not* consider themselves to be salespeople (even though they are). And they had to be very discreet in seeking out referrals from those who were not already patients or clients.

Notice that both groups wanted, needed, and had to have *referrals.* So that word had to be included in my benefit statement, and it had to be plural. They needed continuous, *endless* referrals. Hmm? That's it! My new benefit statement became, "I show people how to cultivate a network of endless referrals."

That benefit statement has become my trademark, and it helped me position myself as an authority in the networking field. And I know it's an effective benefit statement because of the positive comments I receive from those in the mail-order advertising profession.

These people are masters at writing headlines that grab our attention. They *have* to be. After all, they have just split seconds to get us interested enough to keep reading the message. Their "benefits-laden" headlines are often the difference between the successful and unsuccessful advertising campaign. When a prospective mail-order buyer sees that headline, it must immediately present enough of a benefit to get that prospect to continue reading the ad.

Let's Put It Together

Often, a benefit statement will begin along the lines of, "I show people how to..." or "I help people to...." Usually, it isn't a good idea to begin a sentence with the word "I," but in this case we almost have to. If you come up with another beginning that works as well for you, by all means, use it.

What's vital is that you show where you help some*body* do some*thing,* or you do some*thing* for some*body.* That something can be to help them achieve a positive goal or avoid or conquer a particular pain.

One of the best benefit statements I ever heard was from a young man during a seminar in Minneapolis. I was suggesting benefit statements for people in the audience involved in different professions. Somebody then asked me to suggest a benefit statement for stockbrokers, or financial planners. After I gave a few of my standard suggestions, a gentleman named Gregory Zandlo of North East Asset Management raised his hand. He had a benefit statement he'd been using which he thought was also worth mentioning. It was, "We help people create and manage wealth."

Wow! That says it all, doesn't it? How much more effective could a benefit statement possibly be. It's short, sweet, and to the point. It can also fit into any conversation without sounding pushy. And it points out a desire (creating wealth) while solving a problem (managing that wealth).

So follow that lead. Take a moment right now to come up with a benefit statement in the fewest possible words. Do it now. Please do not worry about perfection—just take the first step and put something in writing. Use a separate sheet of paper.

How did you do? It doesn't matter; you are on your way! Keep thinking about it and working on it. Ask those in your network to lend you their ear and provide feedback. Mold this statement. Reshape it. Then memorize it. Internalize your benefit statement so that you know it without first having to think. Then experiment with it and check out responses.

Rick Hill, whom I mentioned earlier, uses what he calls the raised-eyebrow test. According to Rick, "When you tell someone your benefit statement and they start looking around the room for someone else to talk to, you probably need to continue working on it. If, however, they raise their eyebrows with interest and say, `Hmm, tell me more,' you're probably on the right track."

That's as good a description as you'll ever find. And Rick, whose program focuses on prospecting, has an excellent benefit statement himself. When asked what he does, he responds, "I teach companies large and small how to develop a never-ending chain...of new business." Great! And notice the pause after "never-ending chain." "That," says Rick, "is to help that person *literally* picture the never-ending chain."

Let's List a Few More Benefit Statements

The following are just a few benefit statements used by those in particular businesses. A few are repeated from earlier, but I feel it's worth recapping them again.

Chiropractor: I help people heal themselves naturally, without drugs.

Accountant: I give companies large and small timely and accurate financial information while legally minimizing their business and personal tax liability.

Realtor: I help people successfully market their home and buy their perfect dream home.

Financial planner: We help people create and manage wealth.

Advertising agency: We show you how to dramatically increase your company's revenues through strategic positioning in the marketplace.

Life insurance agent: I help people prepare for a sound financial future while protecting themselves and their loved ones for the present.

Graphic artist: I show you how to present your perfect image to those with whom you want to do business.

Solar energy salesperson: We help people save energy and save money all at once through solar heating.

Transactional attorney: Our firm helps people successfully arrange transactions while helping them avoid costly mistakes.

Litigating attorney: Our firm helps people resolve disputes in various forms and avoid costly consequences.

Tell Them How to Know If Somebody *They* Are Talking to Would Be a Good Prospect for *You*

You should take this step *only* when you are sure the other person is ready. If you have already won this person over, they will *want* to network for you. You can come right out and mention to this person that you could use her help.

Because she is grateful for the business you've referred to her, she may actually say to you, "What can I do for you now that you've been such a help to me? You've thrown business at me, you've thought of me. Now what can I do to know if somebody I'm talking to would be a good prospect for you?" This is when we let them know the answer.

If you are a chiropractor, you might respond, "Anyone with neck pain or back pain is a good prospect for me." An accountant might say, "If you know of someone needing help managing the financial end of the business, that person would be a good prospect for me." A banker could suggest that, "A family that mentions adding on to their home would be an excellent prospect for me."

This transaction of information can occur in either a formal or informal session. Since a win-win relationship has been established, there should not be any resentment on the other person's part whatsoever.

One idea is to invite a center-of-influence person you've won over to lunch. Assure her that you look forward to continuing to help her find new business. At the same time, show and teach her how to network for you as well.

How to Ask for Referrals
(So That You Get Them)

Years ago, shortly after I had joined the local sales force of a company, the sales manager held a meeting one morning focusing on how to increase referrals. The question he asked was, "How do you get referrals?" One of the young salespeople who had just come over from another company was supposed to be a real dynamo. He immediately threw up his hands and said, all-knowingly, "You *ask* for them!"

To my amazement, the sales manager said, "That's right." I remember thinking to myself, "How naive!" Actually, they were both half right. You do have to ask. Where they missed the boat, however, is the fact that you have to ask better than that.

Here's why. Have you ever asked someone, either after a sale, or at any other time when you really felt good about this person wanting to help you: "Kay, do you know anybody else who could benefit from my products or services?"

I'll bet Kay began to stare off into space. She was thinking about it—and thinking about it in earnest, really concentrating. Finally, she said, "Well, I can't think of anybody right now, but when I do, I'll definitely let you know." You then probably never heard from her again regarding a referral. And it wasn't Kay's fault.

When we ask people if they "know anyone who..." we are giving them much too large a frame of reference. A blurry collage of 250 faces (their sphere of influence) will run through their mind, but no individual will be singled out. They may feel frustrated, as though they let you down. After everything you've done for them, they feel badly that they can't come through for you as well. It might even make that person feel resentful toward you.

A definite solution to this challenge is to isolate—funnel their world down to just a few people. We've got to give them a frame of reference that they can work with.

Have You Heard the One
about the...

Let me explain it this way. Has anybody ever asked you if you knew any good jokes? Now, you probably know plenty of good jokes, but can you actually think of one when someone asks you? I can't. Here's another example. One night I called my local golden oldies radio station and requested the song "Only in America" by Jay and the Americans. The announcer told me they no longer carry that song on their play list. "But" he asked, "do you happen to know any other oldies you'd like to hear?" I can tell you right now that I know hundreds of oldies I'd like to hear, but could I think of even one at that moment? No way!

It's virtually the same situation when we ask people if they know "anybody" who could benefit from our products or services. Most likely they know plenty of people who could, or who might. Try to get them to think of even one person at that time using that methodology, however, and it's probably not going to happen.

Instead, give them a frame of reference. Let's take the following example. You are talking to Joe, a center of influence in your community. Joe really likes you. You've sent him business, provided him with some background information for one of his projects, and, who knows, maybe you even fixed him up with a blind date that worked out. You are well aware, through asking the right questions during previous conversations, that Joe is a golfing enthusiast and member of his local Rotary Club. Let's see how we can make this situation work.

> YOU: Joe, you were telling me you're an avid golfer.
>
> JOE: Yes, I am. Been playing for over 20 years. If I ever get to retire, I'll probably play every day. Right now, though, it's only on weekends. And I mean, *every* weekend.
>
> YOU: Hmm. Is there a specific foursome you play with most of the time?
>
> JOE: Well, yeah, there's Joe Martin, Ken Stevens, and Nancy Goldblatt.
>
> YOU: Joe, as far as you know, would any of them happen to need...

And then you get into the benefits of what you do. Now, none of the three Joe mentioned might be a good prospect at this particular time, but at least you are increasing his odds of being able to help you. You gave him three people he could *see*. And maybe one or more of them *might* need your product or services. If he tells you, "I'll ask them next time we go out," it may result in some business for you down the line.

Now let's move along to the next frame of reference.

> YOU: How long have you been involved with your local Rotary Club?
>
> JOE: About 6 years now. Great bunch of people.
>
> YOU: Joe, are there one or two people in your club that you tend to sit next to every meeting? (Notice you didn't ask, "Does *anyone* in your club need...")
>
> JOE: Really just one person—Mike O'Brien. Been friends with him and his family for years.
>
> YOU: Has Mike ever mentioned needing a...?

Do you see where we are going with this? The process continues until your networking associate has come up with a few names. Oftentimes, what will happen is this: when one name comes to mind, it will naturally trigger off the names and faces of many others who would also be excellent referrals.

You might be wondering if this will seem pushy. The answer is no, not if this person has genuine good feelings about you and wants to see you succeed. You can also arrive at your meeting with a few names of your own for your friend to call. Nothing at all wrong with doing that.

Keep this in mind: when using this method of asking for referrals, we are, in essence, limiting the number of potential people they might know, but increasing the number of referrals we'll actually receive. Very effective.

One thing I always do is to tell the referrer, "I promise I'll call." And when I call that person, I say, "Hi, Ms. Johnson. This is Bob Burg calling. I *promised* Tom Stevens I'd call you." Sort of positions us a little better in that person's mind right off the bat, doesn't it?

In sales we always want to make it easy for a potential buyer to buy from us. When seeking referrals, we want to make it as easy as possible for a potential referrer to refer to us. Know the frame-of-reference questions you are going to ask *before* you ask them. If *you* feel comfortable with the process, they will too.

Key Points

- We need to train people to know how to network for us.

- Know the difference between features and benefits. A feature is what something *is*, whereas a benefit is what something *does*, or something that solves a problem.

- Develop a benefit statement for the product or service you provide.

- Tell people how to know if someone *they* are talking to is a good prospect for you.

- In order to ask for referrals so that you get them, you must isolate people in the referrer's mind so they can "see" them.

- Isolate people in their mind by giving them a frame of reference.

6

Six Essential Rules of Networking Etiquette

Just like any game, relationship, or business, networking has its rules, procedures, and etiquette. Knowing what to do and following the road map to success is great. Knowing what *not* to do can often be just as beneficial. There really aren't many rules when it comes to networking; however, the few that exist need to be adhered to. If not, there is great risk of destroying the wonderful environment we have created through effective networking.

Don't Ask for Immediate Repayment

When you give something to, or do something for, someone, *do not ask for (or expect) an immediate repayment.* Or a repayment within any time frame at all. We've seen throughout this book how important it is to be a giver. We know that the more we give the more we will receive.

Is there anything more maddening than someone doing something for you, with the unspoken (and sometimes actually spoken) implication, "Now what are you going to do for me?" That isn't networking—it is trading. It is no more than keeping a running tally of who owes what to whom.

Asking for repayment, or letting people know that you feel they *owe* you, will only elicit resentment. Imagine giving someone a lead, a direct referral, or some advice; or maybe you helped their son or daughter get an after-school job at the local hamburger joint. If you then turn around and overtly make that person feel indebted to you, the win-win relationship has been sabotaged. It will only serve as a warning sign to that person that you don't do "something for nothing!"

An incident from my direct sales days immediately comes to mind. I was trying to help a prospect find a product he needed and was having trouble. Suddenly, a man I knew rather indirectly gave me some unsolicited advice on how I could find what I was looking for. Yes, his advice was unsolicited—but extremely helpful.

Later that day he called and asked if his advice was of any help. I told him it certainly was, and that I appreciated his assistance very much. He then politely informed me that, should a sale ensue, he expected a referral fee for his help. I told him that if his advice did lead to a sale, I would honor that, and I said nothing more about it.

The Actual Result, Though, Was Bad Feelings

Needless to say, I very much resented what he did. I decided right then and there I would never ask for or accept his advice again, and I wasn't really anxious to do anything that would benefit him.

Had he not mentioned the referral fee, I would have felt obligated— and even wanted—to return the favor down the road. And knowing how I feel about give and take, you can be certain that what he did for me would have come back to him many, many times over.

Let me clarify something. When I advise you not to make people feel they owe you, I need to qualify that statement. Of course, we want people to feel they owe us, but we want them to *want* to owe us.

When we do something for someone, to help him reach his goals or just to show we care, we elicit good feelings. We foster a mutually beneficial, win-win relationship. That person feels good about us, and either consciously or subconsciously will work hard to give back in kind (if not more).

When we make someone feel threatened or inferior, as though he *owes* us, we cause anger and resentment. In that case, the person may *say* he wants to help us, when in reality, he may want to sabotage our success.

There are times that payback is mentioned by a person as a segue, or bridge, into asking us for help. As wrong as this is, we need to be aware that the person may not feel comfortable asking us for something. In fact, it is more a defense mechanism than anything else.

A fellow speaker was kind enough to send me some information he thought I might find useful. I immediately called to thank him. During our conversation, he discovered that some information I had could be of help to him. Instead of simply asking me to send it, he said, "Listen, since I gave you the other information, would you send this to me?"

Had I not understood his discomfort in making that request, I might have felt resentful. Someone else might actually have been offended and thought, "Oh, so that's why he did that for me." This is the reason we need to be careful in that aspect of networking.

Do something for somebody without the goal being a payback, and you'll usually be paid back anyway. Again and again and again.

Find a Mentor

When seeking a mentor, approach modestly, unassumingly, respectfully, and with the intention of giving more than receiving. A mentor is a person, usually already successful, who wants to take us under his or her wing and help us become a success in our own right. A mentor is the teacher; we are the student.

It's like a good friendship in the way it develops over time. When seeking a mentor, approach modestly, unassumingly, respectfully, and with caution. I've actually heard people just starting in business announce out loud for the world to hear, "I am looking for a mentor." They're probably not going to find one with that approach.

But if you approach your objective correctly, you *can* find people out there who are looking to share their knowledge with an eager young beginner or an eager older professional. You might start by taking them to lunch. (Be sure and pick up the check.) Ask them questions and pick their brains, but do it with sincere respect and appreciation. Make them feel good about the knowledge or skills they possess. But mainly, find out what you can do to help *them*, and then do it!

In many ways, it's similar to what we discussed earlier about cultivating a center-of-influence person to supply you with endless referrals. The same rules apply. You wouldn't walk up to that person and say, "Hi, will you be my unlimited referral source and help me to succeed beyond my wildest dreams?" Of course not. You wouldn't do that in trying to acquire a mentor, either. You've got to establish the relationship gradually, based on mutual give and take, and always try to do more for that person than he or she is doing for you.

Most Mentors *Want* to Be Mentors

Here's the good news: successful people *enjoy* being mentors. They even seek out students. Why? Because it makes an already-made person feel good to share just how he got there, and even to be able to give that student a boost. Mentors want to be remembered fondly by those who follow their advice and go on to be successful themselves.

Ego probably has something to do with it as well. As an established professional speaker, my advice on how to make it in the field of professional speaking is constantly being sought by speakers just starting their careers. And I love to help them. It boosts my ego and allows me to share and teach, which I love to do. And when they become successful and famous, it gives me great pride to know I had a hand in their success.

When I was just beginning in the speaking profession, I was lucky enough to have found the National Speakers Association. Just by joining, I had access to thousands of other professionals. What I found in this benevolent organization was a great bunch of people ready, willing, and able to share their knowledge. You, too, may find it advantageous to join an organization made up of others in your field. It's a good place to find your mentor or mentors. It worked for me.

There isn't any *one* person I would call my mentor, but I can easily think of *several* whom I called constantly with questions. It was amazing the number of questions they answered and the amount of information they shared. Of course, I did the right things as well. I sent a thank-you note after each and every conversation.

Not only that. Whenever I spoke with a prospective client and didn't get the booking, I always made sure to plug one of my mentors. And they knew it. Even though they weren't helping me with the expectation of getting something in return, you can bet that when they saw it happening, it made them feel even better about taking their valuable time in order to help me.

I can genuinely say that much of my quick success as a professional speaker is due to these wonderful people who mentored me, without qualification or reserve. I'm glad I could give something back to them, and I continue to do it now.

One of the nicest compliments I received was after addressing the National Speakers Association at our 1992 national convention in Orlando, Florida. During my speech I hit hard on the importance of finding a mentor and establishing give-and-take relationships. Afterward, numerous members of the audience came up and told me that people who were sitting near, or next to them, had commented out loud, "Burg practices what he preaches. He's referred plenty of business to me."

Keep an Eye on the Clock

When networking, especially if we are asking someone for advice or information, it's extremely important that we respect their time. If I'm calling that person on the phone, the first thing I will always ask is, "Do you have a real quick minute to (answer a question) (give me some advice) (refer me to someone in the widget industry), or is this a lousy time?" If it is a "lousy time," find out when might be a better time. Remember, we want them to feel good about being a part of our network. Wasting their time and not being sensitive to their needs will obviously not help us to accomplish that goal.

Respecting others' time is especially important when contacting someone who doesn't know us personally. Let's take an example. We are considering a direct-mail campaign for our product or service and we realize that before jumping right in, it would be wise to hear some thoughts from someone who's already been there. So we ask someone in our network to connect us with a person he knows in the mail-order industry and he gives us a name.

Imagine how this person would feel if, immediately after our introduction, we started machine-gunning him with question after question after question. How would he feel about our imposing on his time (and expertise) without showing any sensitivity as to his needs? Among those needs is the time he requires to conduct his own business. Every minute he spends answering our questions is a minute away from getting his own job done.

A friend of mine in Philadelphia is a schoolteacher by trade who has amassed a small fortune buying and selling real estate. She went to a lot of seminars, read a lot of books, and suffered numerous setbacks before becoming successful in this venture. People who hear about Sandi will often call her and say that a friend suggested they call and talk to her about investing in real estate.

Enough Is Enough

Knowing Sandi as I do, that is fine. She's a giver and likes to help. Unfortunately, she tells me, most people take advantage of that quality. They will keep her on the telephone for a long time, trying to extract as much information as possible. And, they'll call back time and time again. Eventually, Sandi has to tell them that if they want a *seminar* from her, they'll have to pay.

Imagine people doing that to her—or anyone. How obnoxious! And the truth is, it needn't be that way. Most people love to help and are glad to share what they know. In fact, they want to, if only for ego's sake alone. However, we need to be totally respectful of their time and let them know how much we appreciate it. A little consideration goes a long way.

Follow Through on Promises

One of the more deadly sins of networking is not following through on what we promise to do. Have you ever been exchanging ideas or leads with a fellow networker who has said, "I'll send you that information right away"? After a couple of days, though, the information doesn't arrive. You don't really want to call and remind him because that would appear pushy.

A week later, you still haven't received the information, or even a call from that person. On a scale of 1 to 10, how does that make you feel about that person? How do you rate them for dependability? How much do you trust their word? Also on a scale of 1 to 10, how effective a networker do you feel that person probably is?

Now let's look at a different scenario. Suppose you sell printing, and during a conversation with a fellow networker who's in the business of leasing office space, you learn that a new company will be moving into one of their larger spaces very soon. You recognize the type of business and know they'd be a huge purchaser of printing services. The person with whom you are networking mentions that he'll get you some information on the company and who's who within the organization.

Two days later you receive an envelope with the letterhead of this leasing agent. Upon opening the envelope and pulling out its contents, you notice that the information includes the following: the date the company will be moving in, their purchaser's name and telephone number, and other valuable data that will surely give you the definitive edge over your competition.

Now go back to that 10-point scale and answer those very same questions regarding *this* person. After giving them a score of 10 all around, ask yourself this: Isn't he or she the kind of person you will absolutely go out of your way to help? I know I would, because networkers like that are hard to come by. Also, the more of those types you know and associate with, the more successful *you* are going to be. I guarantee *they* are, and we become like the people with whom we associate.

Be Extra Careful Not to
Annoy a Referred Prospect

Let me paint you a picture of a very ticklish situation. One of your fellow networkers calls you and excitedly says, "I've got someone for you to contact. Our regional manager's name is Carol Davis, and she would be the person with the authority to purchase more of your widgets than you ever thought you could sell to any one company. Just mention my name and she'll take your call."

You like that! In fact, it makes your day—you think. So you eagerly and confidently pick up that ordinarily intimidating instrument known as the telephone and begin dialing. As the secretary begins the screening process, you nonchalantly say, "Just tell her that Dave Smith suggested I call."

Dave Who?

When the secretary questions you as to who Dave Smith would happen to be, you feel a slight pull in your stomach. Something doesn't seem right. Nonetheless, you do not retreat. You say, "Dave is with the Centerville branch of your company." Unimpressed, she puts you on hold and you now find yourself listening to the Musak rendition of "Danke Schoen" over the telephone system. Finally, after about 4 minutes, you are greeted by a somewhat irritated voice. The conversation goes as follows:

CAROL DAVIS: This is Carol Davis.

YOU: Hi, Ms. Davis. This is Joe Taylor calling from Widgets Unlimited.

CD: (silence)

YOU: Uh, Dave Smith referred me to you.

CD: (silence)

YOU: Uh, Dave said you would be the person to speak to regarding the purchasing of widgets for your company.

CD: We don't need any right now. Just send me some information and we'll call you when we're interested.

Obviously, this was not a good referral. At this point I might ask one or two qualifying questions, but if there's any resistance in her voice, I will politely end the conversation.

Although it may be tempting to tell this person to take a long walk off a short pier, it isn't the right thing to do. Such a comment merely serves to lower you to that person's level. Secondly, there's a good chance your return rudeness would get back to Dave, who had given you the referral in the first place.

"So what?" you may be wondering. "It was a terrible, unqualified referral which did me no good at all!" True, but at least he was thinking of you, and, with a little coaching on your part, his future referrals could be all-stars.

Coach Him on How to Help

This goes back to a technique I discussed earlier in the book, and that is training those who network for us. As far as I'm concerned, anyone who refers us once certainly thinks enough of us to give referrals again in the future. If, however, he gets a nasty call from Carol Davis's office or a letter asking him to keep his nose out of corporate headquarters' business, he won't ask you about how rude Carol was. No, he'll assume *you* came on too strong, and he may not risk the prospect of another introduction.

Here's a way to tactfully handle this situation. First, call Dave and thank him very much for thinking of you. Let him know that friends such as him make your job so much easier. Assure him you look forward to referring even more business to him, as well. Then tell him that, as a friend, you feel you should relate to him the circumstances of your contact with Ms. Davis. Let him know that you're telling him this simply for his knowledge, in the event that he may be thinking of referring someone else to Ms. Davis.

In a very matter-of-fact, unemotional manner, review with him your unpleasant conversation with Ms. Davis. Be careful, though. You don't want to embarrass him. Remember, he felt like a big-shot when he gave you the referral ("Just tell her that Dave Smith suggested I call"), so it's imperative you *don't* make him regret that.

Let him know that a similar situation has happened to you, so you can understand and still appreciate his thinking of you. Then just explain that, in future situations, it would probably be helpful to make sure either that the prospect is expecting you to call or that his relationship with the prospect is solid.

Again, it isn't *what* you say but *how* you say it. Using the above as a guideline and spoken with tact (tact—the language of strength), you'll defuse any resentment and turn that lemon into lemonade in the future.

Say (and Write) Thank You

By this time, that should go without saying but it bears repeating anyway. Regardless of whether the lead turns into a huge sale or a bomb like the one in the example above, let that person know how much his thoughts are appreciated.

Another good reason for doing this is to let the referrer know something happened. Once I had to turn down an engagement to speak because I was already booked for that day. Always networking, however, I gave the prospect the name of another speaker who deals with a similar topic. After a week, I realized I had not heard from the other speaker. It wasn't the thank you itself I was after, but the desire to know whether a connection had ever been made. I found out from the *prospect* that it had. Between you and me, I'd have liked the thank you as well. We all like to feel appreciated.

Thanking your referrer is one of those automatics. It never gets tiresome to receive a thank-you note. I have people who consistently refer business to me, and they've made it a point to tell me they *always* appreciate my thank-you notes. I'm convinced it's a major factor in why they continue to refer business my way.

Key Points

In order to maintain and build our network, we must adhere to certain rules of networking etiquette.

- When you give something to or do something for someone, do not ask for (or expect) an immediate repayment.

- When seeking a mentor, approach modestly, unassumingly, respectfully, and with the intention of giving more than receiving.

- Keep an eye on the clock.

- Follow through on promises.

- Be extra careful not to annoy a referred prospect.

- Say (and write) thank you.

7

Prospecting for Fun and Profit

The very first question one might ask when beginning to read this chapter is, "Isn't this entire book about *prospecting?* After all, when we network, aren't we prospecting for business?" Yes—and no. When we network, we are prospecting. When we prospect, however, we aren't necessarily networking.

Let me qualify this statement by explaining that networking and prospecting are like first cousins—same family, but different. In this chapter, we're going to look at prospecting from this angle: Prospecting is getting to the point that the networking relationships begin. Networking, in turn, becomes a vehicle for long-term, lasting results.

Here's a rule to live by:

Never stop prospecting!
Yes, even when we reach the point that all, or almost all, of our business comes from referrals, we continue to prospect within our network.

Let's look at prospecting here as the intangible we've always heard about and most of us have experienced in sales: the endless telephone calls, knocking on doors, and hearing the words, "I'm not interested."

It Doesn't Have to Be That Way

There are ways to prospect that are fun, exciting, and profitable. Sure, you'll prospect by telephone and see people face-to-face. The difference will be in the results, your methods of attaining those results, and your attitude along the way.

You must realize first that sales and prospecting have always been, and always will be, a numbers game. If you make enough calls and see enough people, you will make your share of sales...even if you do things wrong. Of course, the key is to do things right. That way, you'll make more sales in much less time, calling on many fewer people.

A neat formula in practically any type of prospecting takes into account the relationship between calls and contacts, contacts and appointments, and appointments and sales.

For instance, let's say that for every 100 numbers you call (or people/ businesses you call on in person), you actually get to speak or make contact with 40 decision makers. Out of those 40 contacts, you will close 10 appointments. And out of those 10 appointments, you'll make 4 sales.

Letting the numbers and percentages work for us, we realize that every time we call and don't make contact, make a contact but don't get an appointment, or make an appointment but don't close the sale, we're one step closer to success!

That sounds strange, doesn't it? Here's what I mean. You know the chances are 4 in 10 that when you call or visit, you'll contact the right person. If you miss your first one, fine! You've just increased your odds on the next call. If you miss the next, congratulate yourself— you're yet another step closer to your first contact.

Obviously, it isn't quite that simple. The numbers work over a long period of time. Nonetheless, the more calls in which you don't hit your goal (contacting the right person), the greater your odds that the next one will be it.

How to Put a Dollar Value on Small Failures

Let's take those same 100 calls and the same ratios. Let's say in this scenario that each closed sale makes you $300 in commission. If it's going to take 100 total calls to make four sales ($1200), then can't we break that down into $12 per call? That's right! Every time you pick up the phone or visit a business or knock on a door, you net $12. If you can't make the initial contact, that's $12. If you make the initial contact but can't close the appointment and can't close the sale, that's $12. When someone says, "I'm not interested!!!!" simply say (to yourself), "That's $12, please."

How to Prospect Yourself into a Raise

You can raise your salary one of two ways: by making more calls or by turning a higher percentage of initial calls into contacts, contacts into appointments, and appointments into sales. That's what we'll discuss for the remainder of this chapter. We'll look at effective ways of prospecting, individually and both, by telephone and by visiting in person.

Turn Your Telephone into $$$

It's understandable that the telephone can be an intimidating object. After all, people can be rude, which means prospects can be rude. We realize that when we make prospecting calls, we are probably taking people away from something they are already doing to increase their own business. Since they don't yet know the benefits of our products or services, they may not like that. Their resentment might come across to us in a most obvious way.

If you are like me, you are naturally sensitive to rejection. Hey, I like to be liked! It isn't fun when people say they're not interested, or hang up the phone, or fib to quickly rid themselves of our pesky presence. But realizing that this is the worst-case scenario and that their rejection isn't personal (after all, they've never met us), we can now turn these calls into the beginnings of making money.

Let me point out something right now about using the telephone. Depending upon your particular business, you might be using the telephone simply to get in-person appointments. That is the usual case. In direct sales we had a saying that you never tried to sell your product on the telephone. The only thing you tried to close on the telephone was the in-person appointment!

There are businesses, however, where the telephone is used both to prospect *and* to close the sale. As a professional speaker, my business definitely fits that description. After all, if my marketing staff or I had to visit meeting planners and decision makers all over the country in order to close a booking, we'd spend much more time in travel and money in travel-related expenses than we could ever recoup by actually speaking and marketing our books and tapes.

Other businesses fall into that category as well, so I'll discuss this aspect of teleprospecting before talking about phone techniques for simply closing the appointment.

As I've shared at live seminars the techniques my staff and I use to prospect and sell by telephone, I've heard from many people selling numerous other products and services that these techniques work for them as well. So as you read how we do it, simply imagine how you can bend and twist the techniques to your own unique situation.

"Know You, Like You, Trust You" Is Even More Important Now

Probably the most difficult aspect of teleprospecting is that you are not right in front of the person during your presentation. There is less control in this situation because you can't read their facial expression and body language and you don't know if they are giving the conversation their undivided attention or working on something else while you're speaking to them.

And it is certainly easier for someone to get rid of us on the telephone than it is in person. After all, what's to keep that person from saying, "Listen, something just came up and I have to go. I'll call you if I'm ever in need of your product." Sure she will—in your dreams.

So, needless to say, establishing a relationship with this person based on good feelings is essential right from the start. And this process begins with the secretary, especially if that person has assumed, or been asked to assume, the role of screener or gatekeeper.

Find the Person Who Can Say Yes

The first thing we need to do is make sure we are asking for the right person, the decision maker. We can do a wonderful job of getting past the secretary, make a great impression on the person to whom we are presenting, and close the sale beautifully. If, however, the person we've just sold on our product or service does not have the authority to say yes, we've wasted our time (as well as hers).

In many instances, it is obvious who the decision maker is. In that situation, you already have a step up. But let's take a look at various ways to qualify a prospect before we go too far into the presentation.

First might be the receptionist. Sometimes receptionists don't know who the actual decision makers are, but usually they do, or at least they can refer you to someone who knows. When calling a corporation or association to book a speech, I will say to the receptionist, "Good morning, my name is Bob Burg. Who's the person in charge of hiring outside professional speakers for your annual convention?" In your case, the proper question might be, "Good morning, this is Jane McGregor. Who's the person in charge of purchasing widgets?" Or handling advertising? Or purchasing office products? Same thing, right?

That question will send me in the right direction. I'll then ask to be transferred to the decision maker's office, realizing I'll probably get his or her secretary. *Warning:* If the person answering the phone is the secretary or wants to know why you are calling, find a reason to politely get off the telephone (after, of course, finding out the information you wanted). When speaking with the person who'll decide whether or not to screen us or put us through, we need to already have that information and appear to be "in the know."

Getting Past the Gatekeeper

Let's pretend that the decision maker is Mary Jones and her secretary is Julie Smith. Julie answers the phone.

JULIE: Good morning, Mary Jones's office. May I help you?

ME: (informal and friendly, as though I belong) Good morning, this is Bob Burg. May I speak with Mary, please?

JS: And where are you calling from, Mr. Burg?

She wants to know the name of our company, doesn't she? That way, she can decide if what we do will be of interest to Mary or if she should discourage us. What I'll do at this point is answer with the name of my city, and then segue right into a reflexive closing question, "What's your name?"

JS: And where are you calling from, Mr. Burg?

ME: Jupiter, Florida—I'm sorry, what's your name?

JS: Julie Smith.

ME: Oh, thank you, Julie.

Notice there was no pause between "Jupiter, Florida" and "I'm sorry, what's your name?" I didn't want to give her an opportunity to say, "No, I mean what company are you with?" Instead I went right into my reflexive closing question, "What's your name?"

A *reflexive closing question* is simply a question that produces an automatic response. When asked, "What is your name?" most people respond reflexively. Hopefully, she will put us through at that point. Does that technique work every time? No! It works some of the time.

If, instead, she says, "No, I mean, what company are you with?" or "What's your call in reference to?" you need to have a short statement which says just enough to raise her interest and position your call as worthwhile enough to be put through, but not enough to say what it is you actually do.

I might say, "This regards your upcoming convention. Mary would be in charge of profit-making programs, wouldn't she?" If you sell computer systems you might say, "I can show her how to dramatically increase her department's profitability for little cost. Julie, I'll explain to her just how to do that."

Does this technique work every time? No! It works some of the time. Let's say that in this case it didn't work and Julie wouldn't put you through. Or possibly, Mary isn't in. Make sure you've written down Julie's name, because you will use her name as a positioning tool for credibility on your next call, which is a few days later. After all, you don't want to go through the same song and dance again.

> JS: Good morning, Mary Jones's office. May I help you?
>
> ME: (very friendly) Hi, Julie?
>
> JS: Yes.
>
> ME: (very friendly) Julie, hi! This is Bob Burg, how are you?
>
> JS: (wondering who the heck Bob Burg is) Uh, f-fine, and you?
>
> ME: Great. Hey, is Mary in?

Keep in mind that Julie talks to many people every single working day. She can't possibly recall every person and conversation. Also remember that, although it may be Julie's job to screen calls, it isn't her job to keep people from getting through who *should* be put through. In this scenario, I sound as though I belong. As though I've been there before. Does this technique work every time? No! It works some of the time.

There are many ways to get past the gatekeeper. I come across more and more of them every day in various books and sales newsletters and at seminars I attend. Not every idea will work for you, or for me, but some will. Let me share just a couple of techniques that have consistently worked for me.

Try These—They Work!

The first technique is use of priority mail, available from your local post office. For $2.90 (at the time of this book) you can send a letter to the decision maker in a huge, attention-getting, red, white, and blue cardboard envelope. Usually, because of the perceived value of this package (it *must* be important if it was sent priority mail), it will, in fact, get in front of the boss.

Inside this huge, multicolored, cardboard envelope is your letter enclosed in a regular number 10 envelope. It should be brief, businesslike, and to the point. It should let the person know who you are and should also contain a short benefit statement and a request to be put through next time you call. Here's a generic example:

Dear Mr. Thomas,

Would you like to know more about a sure-fire way to cut down on your sales staff's wasted, nonproductive time? Gadger Gidgets. These profit builders, designed specifically for your particular industry, will show you how to increase production and profitability by up to 34 percent, and at a very affordable price.

When I've called, you've been very busy. I'm sure that's the norm for you. May I make a request? I'll call Thursday, October 17, at 2:10 p.m. If you are in, I'd appreciate your taking my call. I promise to be brief and help you determine quickly if our system may fit your needs.

If you are not in and would like to speak with me, could you have your secretary schedule a time for me to call back at your convenience.

Sincerely yours,

Steve Larkin

One quick point: notice that the time I gave was 2:10 p.m. Whenever scheduling any appointment you should suggest an odd time, as opposed to 2:00, 2:15, 2:30, or 2:45. This gives the impression of your time being clearly slotted, accounted for, and important. The same goes for percentages: 34 percent is actually much more credible than 35 percent. Why? Because it's much more specific, and it suggests documentation.

By the way, you should only say that if it is a fact. And if the exact percentage result was 35 percent, you're *still* better off going with 34 percent. But if increased production and productivity are not at least 34 percent, absolutely don't state that.

Back to your letter. If Mr. Thomas is impressed by the possible benefits mentioned in your letter, he'll take your call. If not, it is up to you to decide whether to blow that one off or try another tack. Here's a technique that I learned from Harvey Mackay's book *Swim with the Sharks without Being Eaten Alive*. In it, Mackay tells how to get to the person he calls the "tough prospect," the one who won't take your calls. Mackay's technique (which I am loosely paraphrasing in this explanation) can also be used as a way of getting past the screen. This has earned positive results for my staff and myself on numerous occasions. Here's how.

Simply put a money value on the time you'll take to speak with the decision maker. The following example is a conversation I had with a secretary who had consistently denied me access to the boss for over 3 weeks. After reading Mr. Mackay's book, I decided to go for it.

ME: May I speak with Mr. Prospect, please?

SECRETARY: No, he's busy.

ME: May I make a telephone appointment to speak with him?

SECRETARY: No, he's too busy even for that. Just send whatever it is you have in writing! (charming individual)

ME: I'll tell you what. Please put me on hold and ask Mr. Prospect if I can take just 200 seconds of his time. Tell him that if I go even 1 second over, I'll donate $500 to his favorite charity.

SECRETARY: (bewildered) Hold on a moment.

COMPANY MESSAGE OVER EASY LISTENING BACKGROUND MUSIC: "You'll find this to be one company that really loves people." (The message was actually pretty close to that.)

SECRETARY: He'll take your call at 9 tomorrow morning...and his charity is the Heart Fund.

TELEPHONE: Click!

Nonetheless, at least I got to speak to the decision maker. As an offshoot to this story, I have found that this technique works quite often, and most secretaries are happy to go along with it. Also, in many cases, the decision maker will come right to the phone, probably curious as to what kind of person would make that kind of statement. Again, does it work all of the time? No, but I can guarantee it will *never* work if you don't try it.

Before going on to our conversation with the decision maker, I ask you to keep this in mind: always be pleasant to the secretaries, and realize that they are just doing their job. Maybe a bit overzealously, yet we're not going to win them over by being testy or argumentative. We have to make these "key" people our friends. We do that by being courteous, using their names, finding mutual points of interest, and establishing a rapport.

Now You've Got the Decision Maker

Okay, so I've been put through to Mary Jones. She is the decision maker who could hire me to do a networking speech or seminar. You'll have to take this example and modify it to accomplish what you want to accomplish with *your* product or service.

MARY JONES: Hi, this is Mary Jones. How can I help you?

ME: Good morning, Ms. Jones (not "Mary" yet), this is Bob Burg. I understand you're the person in charge of hiring outside professional speakers for your annual convention. Is that correct?

MJ: Yes, it is. What can I do for you?

ME: Well I...by the way, do you have a real quick minute?

There are those from the "old school of sales" who will probably groan as they read the words, "do you have a real quick minute?" I can almost hear them say, "Burg, why on earth would you ask a person that question? You're just giving them an excuse to say they're busy and get rid of you!"

Here's what I've found in my 10 years of teleprospecting experiences. People generally will answer that question in one of three ways:

Number 1: "No!" Actually, that answer will probably be more along the lines of, "No I don't have a minute. I don't have any time at all. I'm between meetings, trying to make a deadline, and I especially don't have time to talk to anyone who wants to sell me anything."

As far as I'm concerned, that answer is fine. They are letting us know in no uncertain terms that this would not be a good time. We won't have their full, or even partial, attention. Trying to share the benefits of our product or service with them now would only bring about resentment from their end, destroying any chance of establishing a relationship with them. Our job at this time is to politely get off the phone. We'll try again later.

Number 2: "Yes." I know that sounds good. If, however, that "yes" is followed by, "I've got all the time in the world. I'm not doing anything anyway. What can I do for you?" then be warned: that person is probably not the decision maker.

I say this only somewhat tongue-in-cheek. There are people out there in nonpower positions who like to play king for a day. They will lead you on forever, yessing you to death. Then, when it's time to take action, they have no authority. I speak from experience. It's happened to me!

Number 3: "Yes, real quick." Typically, the response might be more like, "I have a *real* quick minute, but that's it. I'm very busy." As negative as that may sound, that is exactly the response you want.

At this point, we'll give them a quick benefit statement. This benefit statement will, of course, explain the benefits of what they can expect by doing business with us, without telling them enough to make an instant decision to say no. When they respond positively, we will then be in a position to take control of the conversation. And you know that we don't take control by telling, but by asking questions. Remember, no one is going to hang up the phone on you while *they* are talking.

ME: Well I...by the way, do you have a real quick minute?

MJ: Real quick, I'm very busy. What can I do for you?

ME: I do a program entitled "How to Cultivate a Network of Endless Referrals." Does that sound like a program that may be of value at your next convention?

Usually, the prospects I call will answer yes. That's because before I target a particular market, I qualify the "need it" and "want it" aspect of that market. [There are three parts to what is known as the marketing bridge we all need to cross when working with prospects: (1) Do they need it? (2) Do they want it? (3) Can they afford it?] Whether or not they can afford my fee will often need to be determined later.

If you are in a business where you can prequalify the wants and needs of your market, great. If not, you'll have to make a few more calls in order to qualify the same number of prospects.

Obviously, you'll want to come up with a benefit statement that works as well for you as mine does for me. If the prospect does show interest, it might be appropriate (depending upon the situation, you may need to wait) to further qualify her position by asking, "Mary, along with you, who else will be in on the decision-making process?" That, of course, is much more tactful than saying, "Are you really the decision maker, or are you just pulling my leg?"

Again, tongue-in-cheek, but understand the difference. The first way of asking shows respect and gives our prospect an *out* without causing her embarrassment. And it lets you know that there are other people to whom you may have to make your presentation. If you come right out and ask if your prospect is actually the decision maker, she might have to say yes in order to save face. By the time she finally admits she is not, 3 months have gone by. Again, that will only waste your time and your prospect's time.

Where the Selling Process Actually Begins

From this point on it is now a matter of making a good presentation by asking questions to determine wants and needs, being able to answer objections, and closing the sale. After qualifying and question asking, you should have a good idea of what you need to do for the next telemeeting. If you need to send information to your prospect before speaking with her again, take the proper steps to ensure she will receive your material and actually review it before your next call.

Jeff Slutsky recommends describing to prospects in detail the type of package and envelope they will receive, including size, color, and insignias or logos. Then you must get a commitment from them that they'll review your information. After determining with your prospect the exact day and time you will have your follow-up conversation, I suggest words along the lines of, "Mr. Dennison, many people, after reviewing the information, have questions on two key points, the whichamacallit and the whichamahoozie. I'll look forward to discussing those points with you."

That day, send a note on your personalized postcard as discussed earlier in the book. If you have your picture on it, prospects will feel more like they know you and will be more comfortable in doing business with you. And, if nothing else, it will remind them that you were serious about getting back in touch and expecting them to have reviewed your material.

Since the focus of this book is not sales presentation skills or how to close the sale, I suggest you turn to other sources on these subjects and learn the proper techniques that will best suit you and your prospects, customers, and clients.

There are many excellent books on the market today regarding these skills, and some to keep away from. Two books I strongly urge you to purchase and devour are *Secrets of Closing the Sale* by Zig Ziglar and *How to Master the Art of Selling* by Tom Hopkins. Both books are packed with real-world knowledge, and they dispel the myth of the "born salesperson."

Contrary to popular belief, people are not born salespeople, nor are they born closers. Selling and closing are both developed, learned skills. An art and a science. Both authors are excellent at each, and I personally give them a lot of credit and thanks for helping me become the salesperson I have become. Their books are listed in the resource section at the conclusion of this book.

Selling the Appointment by Telephone

Ironically enough, even though most people use the telephone simply to set appointments, this section of the chapter will be brief. Here's why: the toughest part is still just getting to the decision maker. You've already learned how to do that!

Now it's simply a matter of closing the appointment. If you are involved with a product that must be demonstrated or explained in person, do *not* get sucked into giving your presentation over the telephone. It won't work, especially for high-ticket items. When I was selling solar energy systems, which averaged around $10,000 per unit, I was constantly asked on the phone how much it cost. Can you imagine answering "$10,000" without first their knowing the benefits of what the system would do for them and how much they would actually save? Depending upon the individual family, water usage, and home, and available tax credits, these solar energy systems were of enormous value. But do you think a salesperson ever got the chance to come over and explain that once they divulged the price? No way!

If this is the case with your product or service, you need to have a learned, memorized response for every question or objection you will receive on the way to setting that appointment. Price won't be the only one. If you are worried that your presentation will sound "canned," have no fear.

If you practice beforehand to the point that the information is internalized, your responses will sound completely natural. Think of stage, television, and movie actors and actresses. They would never imagine just getting up there and winging it.

Again, when first speaking with decision makers, you must hit them with a benefit statement (even if it's in the form of a question) that will pique their interest without giving away too much information. Then, after a brief presentation or several qualifying questions, go into closing for the appointment. If I were selling a solar energy system, the conversation might go as follows:

ME: Hi, Ms. Prospect, this is Bob Burg. Do you have a real quick minute?

PROSPECT: It depends. What do you need?

ME: I'm with Sunstrong Solar Energy Company. May I ask you just a very few questions regarding the rising of your monthly hot water bills? (If rising hot water bills are a concern for that prospect, the answer will probably be yes).

After a few more questions enhancing the prospect's interest, it is time to set the in-home appointment. It might, however, not go without a couple of questions or objections from them.

PROSPECT: Before we waste each other's time, how much does your system cost?

ME: Good question, and very important. It really depends on several things. Every home and family is different, and has its own individual needs. The nice thing is that it's my job to see that *your* needs will be met.

Now go into closing for the appointment. It has been taught for years that the best way to do this is to give the prospect a choice of two yeses, as opposed to a yes or a no. In other words, if we ask, "Would Tuesday evening at 8 be good for you?" the prospect might say no. Now we have to guess on another convenient date and time. "How about Wednesday at 7?" to which the prospect responds, "Naw, that's no good either. I'll tell you what, let me think about it for a while, and if I'm interested I'll get back to you." At that point you've probably lost your prospect.

Instead, we give them a choice of two yeses.

> ME: Would tomorrow evening at 7:15 be good, or would Wednesday evening at 7:45 be more convenient for you?
>
> PROSPECT: Tomorrow's no good. I guess we can do it Wednesday.

This technique is called the "alternate of choice." It's very effective, yet we need to be careful when using it for two reasons. First, people are more educated to sales techniques, and this one has been around for a while. Second, if you phrase the alternate of choice the same way too many times it *sounds* salesy and manipulative.

Instead, let it flow with genuine concern regarding the convenience of your prospect. If he or she fires another question or objection at you, simply respond and go back into another alternate-of-choice question in order to set the appointment.

Listening Is the Key

Whether using the telephone as a complete sales tool or simply to get appointments, the key to success is having a game plan, following it religiously, and listening to your prospect. Fellow speaker Jim Meisenheimer, who specializes in personalized sales training programs, recommends the following 10 tips for telephone success:

1. *Prepare in advance.* Prepare your questions and responses in advance. Know your product or service well, and your mind will be free to listen to the customer and focus on his or her needs.

2. *Limit your own talking.* You can't talk and listen at the same time. Jim makes an excellent point. We have a saying at my company: "If *we* are doing the talking, nothing is being sold."

3. *Focus.* Concentrate on your conversation and the customer's needs. This means temporarily shutting out your personal problems and worries. Difficult at times but possible, and definitely necessary.

4. *Put yourself into your prospect's shoes.* Understand their needs and concerns by thinking like them. Take their point of view in order to help them solve their problems.

5. *Ask questions.* We know the importance of asking questions during a presentation. Asking questions will also help clear up any points or prospect concerns you are not sure you completely understand. Paraphrasing the prospect's concerns back to them in the form of a question, followed by, "Do I understand you correctly?" or, "Is that what you're saying?" will keep you on the right track.

6. *Don't interrupt.* Nothing will turn a prospect off quicker than interrupting them. The same goes for finishing their sentences for them. Don't assume you know what they are going to say (even if you have to bite your lip to keep from doing it). Jim also suggests that just because the person pauses, he or she is not necessarily through talking.

7. *Listen for the whole idea or complete picture.* Words alone are not necessarily conveying what your prospect fears or desires.

8. *Respond (as opposed to react) to the ideas—not to the person.* Don't allow yourself to become irritated or insulted. Objections and questions are not personal. Also, don't let a prospect's mannerisms, such as an accent, distract you.

9. *Listen between the lines.* Often, what is *not* said by the prospect is just as important as what is said. Listen for overtones, doubts, concerns.

10. *Use interjections.* Show the customer you are listening by occasionally saying, "Uh-huh," "I understand what you're saying," "I see what you mean," or other fillers. Don't overdo it, though.

Several Quick, Final Tips for the Telephone

Use a mirror to check your attitude. Every telemarketing authority I know will always suggest hanging a mirror on the wall in front of you so you can see yourself as you converse. Why? Because your mood and attitude absolutely *will* come across to your prospect. If the reflection in the mirror is up and smiling, that's how you'll come across on the telephone. The opposite is also true.

Be careful with the hold button. If you must put a person on hold, do so for as short a time as possible—15 to 30 seconds, no more. If you leave prospects on any longer, you'll notice a change in *their* attitude, and it won't be for the better. To better understand why, notice what happens when you are the one stuck on hold for any length of time. It's frustrating, and definitely not fun.

In fact, try this experiment. Glance at your watch and notice the second hand. Then sit there doing nothing for about 2 minutes, and then glance back at your watch. As long as the time seems, it probably won't even come close to 2 minutes.

Hang up last. One definite fact of life is that none of us likes the cold sound of the "click" in our ear. When you hear that awful sound, don't you sometimes feel as though the person was in a hurry to get rid of you and go on to the next person? That's how your prospect might feel as well. Let her hang up first.

Finding Prospects from Conventional and Unconventional Sources

The key to effective prospecting is to work smarter, not harder—to get yourself in front of qualified people with the least amount of time and effort. There are just a few methods for accomplishing that goal.

Physically Position Yourself in front of the Right People

Speaker and author Rick Hill says, "If you're going to go fishing, go where the fish are." Makes sense, doesn't it? The same could be said about prospecting for gold, meeting members of the opposite sex, and prospecting for new business.

Back when Rick was setting records as a radio advertising sales representative, he used to leave his office at 2 p.m. every Friday. When his sales manager would ask where he was going, Rick would give him the name of a local watering hole. When the manager questioned him as to why he was doing this before the workday ended, Rick would reply, "How are my sales this month?" At that, the manager would stop his questioning.

Actually, Rick was going to the local club where advertising agency representatives hung out on Friday afternoons. Rick couldn't have put his prospects in front of him any better if he had sprung for an elaborate party.

Ask yourself where your prospects hang out. Are there certain clubs, organizations, and associations you could join that would give you continuous access to these people? If so, invest some time and money and join. The dividends will more than justify the expense.

Find the Orphans

When you begin with a new company, or even if you have been there for some time, realize that every time a salesperson leaves the company, he or she leaves behind a number of customers and clients that are no longer being serviced. They are your orphans.

If your product is one that can be purchased again or upgraded—a car, a computer system, or a copying machine—contact that customer and establish a relationship. One copying machine salesperson was referred to as "Mr. Upgrade." That's because as soon as he joined the company, he began calling orphans and talking to them about upgrading their present system. From what I understand, he did extremely well.

When I joined the solar energy company, I used orphans as sources of referrals, since their systems should last for life (no resales) and upgrades are seldom. I'd introduce myself and ask how happy they were with their system. Since the product was great, I could count on many ecstatic answers. I'd then ask for referrals of those they knew who might also be able to benefit from a similar system. Did it work all of the time? No, but it worked a lot of the time. Use your imagination and always wonder how you can assist someone in meeting *their* needs. Zig Ziglar says, "You can get everything in life you want if you just help enough other people get what they want."

What's the Itch Cycle?

I first learned about this great idea from Tom Hopkins. Statistics will show that, depending upon the product, there is an average time expectancy between purchases. In other words, a time length before one itches to buy again. For instance, the average home owner will move every 5 years. The average new car buyer will buy every 2 to 3 years.

Go back to the orphans again. How long has it been since they last purchased? What is the average itch cycle for that product? Have they purchased more than once? If so, what was their time frame, or itch cycle, between purchases?

Look in Local Newspapers

It was mentioned earlier in the book that we should always scour the newspaper for information of interest to those in our network. That way, we let them know we care and that they are on our mind—a very effective networking technique.

The newspaper can also be used as an excellent prospecting tool. For instance, if you are a life or health insurance sales professional and read about someone receiving a big promotion, don't you think his or her insurance needs to be increased? What about people who have a new baby? Check out those birth announcements! Find out where they live and send them a congratulatory note. Maybe they have an insurance person already—but then again, maybe they don't. Or possibly their insurance agent doesn't pay attention to those things and you do. A nice congratulations note and follow-up phone call could work wonders, couldn't it?

If you are in real estate, you know where to find the "For Sale By Owners" list in the classified section. Get up a little earlier than your competition and make your calls. Find out the owners' address and get yourself over there. Be nice, nonpushy, and caring about their needs. Once you've established a rapport, begin doing the things you've learned in this book about networking and cultivating relationships.

Go Door-to-Door, Business-to-Business

Although this method is the most time-consuming, it is very effective for this reason: whenever you make your contact with the decision maker, you are in the very best position to establish the rapport necessary to close the sale.

Again, depending upon your particular business, your sales might be of the one-call, two-call, or several or more calls variety. Regardless, getting in front of your prospects cuts out every other step in between. You can read their body language, gather your facts, and answer objections without their having a quick escape. The more people you see face-to-face, the more sales you will make and the more lives you will enhance.

A Lesson on How *Not* to Prospect Door-to-Door

Davis Fisher is a training consultant for SDA Corporation in Rolling Meadows, Illinois. At a recent speaking engagement I had in Chicago, he shared the following story with me.

> Our offices are located in a 10-story building, not too far from O'Hare International Airport. For some reason we are in a perfect location for salespeople who make cold calls. A few years ago there was a unique moment in the day when I was in the office alone. It was around noontime. The receptionist had stepped down the hall and our coworkers were either at lunch, on errands, or out of town.
>
> A knock on the door. "Come in," I said, and in walked a young

salesman. He said to me, "Do you have a minute?" and I said, "Sure." And with that he pulled up a chair, sat down at my desk, opened his briefcase, pulled out some brochures, moved a couple things on my desk, and spread the brochures out.

For the next 13½ minutes we went through his brochures. He told me all about what he was selling—computers for the small office. I sat there looking at his brochures, nodding my head, saying "Uh-uh," "Ooooh," "That's a big one," "Wow," "Color on that one's neat."

At the end of the 13½ minutes, he picked up his brochures, put them back in his briefcase, set it down next to him, looked around, and said, "Nice office you have here." I said, "Thank you." He looked over my shoulder through a big picture window looking out on the spaghetti bowl intersection of a major expressway and toll road. He said, "Wow, you really have a view of the toll road from here." I said, "Yeh, we do." He looked at me and asked, "What do you folks do here?" I replied, "We teach people how to sell." "No kidding," he replied. "How am I doing?" And I said, "Not very well."

Why not? Because in his 15-minute sales call, this salesperson spent 13½ minutes telling me how much he knew about what he was selling. He never asked me any questions. Had he asked, he would have discovered that we had bought a computer for our office 6 months earlier and had no immediate need.

At that point he might have asked questions such as, "No kidding, what kind did you get? How did you happen to go with them? What's been your experience over the last 6 months? Who was involved in making that decision? If you were going to make that decision today, what would be different about it? I realize that you are tied into a contract now with those people, Mr. Fisher, but let me leave a brochure describing several of our products, including one here that I think may give you some assistance based on some of the problems you have had.

"Feel free to give me a call over the next three months in the event I may help you out. In fact, if I haven't heard from you, may I call you? Do you have a brochure describing what you do? I always like to know what some of my prospective clients do. Possibly I can refer some business your way. May I have one of your cards? Thanks...I'm curious: do you know of anyone in the area who might be in a similar position to the one you were in 6 months ago, so I might talk to them and see if I may be of some assistance? Thanks. Bye."

And then leave—saving himself 13½ minutes on a 15-minute sales call so that he could use that valuable time down the hall or across the street where he might encounter someone who, indeed, could become a qualified prospect based on appropriate probing and listening! Good selling is not telling!

Davis makes an excellent point. The worst thing a salesperson can do is simply walk in, introduce himself, sit down without being invited to do so, and start "machine-gunning" through a presentation. If faced with the decision maker, we must first discover (or create) a need, a want, and a financial capability.

With just a bit of questioning, the salesperson in the above example would have discovered earlier that there was no need. With some creative questioning, however, he also could have discovered the prospect's itch cycle, and maybe even picked up a few referrals along the way. As professionals, we don't want to waste our prospects' time. We don't want to waste our time, as well.

Some Thoughts on Effective Prospecting

A friend of mine, Sonia Cooper, is a salesperson and prospector par excellence. Her motto is, "Put the needs of your customers/prospects/referral sources first...and your paycheck will follow." A few years back Sonia was an account representative for a title insurance company. One day she noticed a real estate agent from the neighboring county stuffing the mailboxes in a real estate office in the county where she worked.

Sonia felt that as a commercial real estate broker he had better things to do than travel office to office (which Sonia did as part of her job), so she offered to pass out his fliers for him since she'd be there anyway. To which title account representative do you think that commercial broker referred his title orders from resulting sales? The answer should be obvious.

A true believer in self-promotion and "keeping your name and telephone number in front of prospects," she constantly looks for new and creative ways to accomplish this goal. Once, when she was on a cruise ship, she noticed that each day the crew would pass out word games for the passengers to solve. Each day was a different theme.

She had the social hostess put together a packet of all 12 games and the answers—not knowing exactly how she would use them. Upon returning to work, she came up with the idea of passing out the word quiz to all of her individual prospective agents. Each month, on appropriately colored paper, she would distribute her and her firm's name along with a different word quiz. Answers to the previous month's quiz were on the back.

According to Sonia, this was a huge hit. In a very subliminal way, they saw her name and phone number all month long. They were especially effective during normally slow times. Instead of just sitting around doing nothing and waiting for the phone to ring, her prospects were actively having fun with her word quizzes. Some of the offices actually had internal contests as to which agent could come up with the most correct answers. According to Sonia, "This was one of the most inexpensive and successful prospecting promotions I ever implemented."

Sonia is now an account executive with BellSouth Communications, Inc. in West Palm Beach, Florida. Upon joining the company, she got off to another impressive start, racking up huge sales numbers. Sonia knocks on a lot of business doors and is often faced with having to get past the gatekeeper. She has six techniques she uses with great success:

1. *Treat them like they own the company.* Not only because one day they might, but they are probably the person their boss looks to for protection from the outside world. If you can make them feel good about themselves, they'll help you do the same, by ensuring you get to see the decision maker.

2. *Know them by their first name.* Show them that they are important to you by using their name.

3. *Tell them that you need their "help."* The fact is, most people want to help, and to feel that you know they have the power to help.

4. *Include them in the promotional materials you pass out.* Keep them in the loop. Make them a part of the sales process.

5. *Put yourself in their shoes.* How would you like to be treated in the same position? Respect them as people, unlike other salespeople who treat them like nonentities whose sole purpose in life is to keep the salesperson from achieving his or her goal of seeing the decision maker.

6. *Be of service to them.* Ask them if there isn't any way you can help them—maybe drop something off at the post office for them on your way there?

And of course, make them your ally. Smile, be sincere, and appreciate the importance of the job they have to do.

Pat Hance, broker-owner of Pat Hance Real Estate Company in Plantation, Florida, feels it's very important, when prospecting, to continually have your name out to the public. She believes that everyone she meets, anywhere, is either a prospect or an excellent source of referrals.

Pat is also an expert at prospecting other Realtors. She attends every real estate convention she possibly can, handing out a flyer with her photo on it, containing the words, "Pat Hance wants your referrals!" in huge print. She says consistency is important, keeping the same message year after year after year, making only minor changes to show additional designations and honors she's received.

In Pat's own words, "This little flyer has been given to every attendee at every real estate convention since 1969. Do they remember me? You bet! I've received comments when the new updated photo replaces the less recent one (e.g.: I see you're no longer using your high school photo).

"I've received referrals from agents I've never met—agents who received this flyer somehow, somewhere. It's not important that they remember how or where, just that they remember Pat Hance!"

After discovering that a New York ERA real estate office had blown up her picture to poster size and tacked it up on the bulletin board, she arranged a neat cross-promotion with that office's broker. When he visited Florida on vacation, he took a video recorder to Pat's office and taped her saying, "Come on to Florida. Send your buyers! Send your sellers! We want to work for you in sunny, south Florida." This resulted in numerous sales and referrals for Pat.

Pat considers herself the biggest "flesh presser" of them all, meeting people in all walks of life, from the supermarket to her church. Yet, wherever and whenever she does this, she focuses on the other person's needs, not her own. She knows that eventually, with the way she is positioned and known in her community, that person will remember her when the time is right for business or referrals. One introduction and handshake, through the twists of fate, resulted in referral fees on approximately 35 transactions over the course of several years.

Yes, whether prospecting by telephone or in person, the basic rules apply. Follow the road map, be creative at times, and most of all, always have the other person's wants and needs in the forefront of your mind.

Key Points

- Never stop prospecting.

- Prospecting is a numbers game. The more things we do right, however, the more sales we will get in less time and after calling on fewer people.

- There is a definite relationship between calls and contacts, contacts and appointments, and appointments and sales. Learn yours and use it to your advantage.

- When using the telephone as a prospecting tool, establishing a relationship with that prospect becomes even more important.

- Knowing how to talk to (and get past) the gatekeeper is vital to teleprospecting success.

- Ask the prospect, "Do you have a real quick minute?"

- Qualify to ensure you are speaking with the decision maker!

- Use your short benefit statement to pique prospects' interest so they'll want to hear more.

- If using the telephone simply to set in-person appointments, be sure to limit your conversation to just that. Give too much information and you may disqualify yourself right then and there.

- Utilize the following tips from Jim Meisenheimer:
  1. Prepare in advance.
  2. Limit your own talking.
  3. Focus. Concentrate on your conversation and the customer's needs.
  4. Put yourself into your prospects' shoes. Understand their needs and concerns by thinking like them. Take their point of view in order to help them solve their problems.
  5. Ask questions.
  6. Don't interrupt.
  7. Listen for the whole idea or complete picture. Words alone are not necessarily conveying what your prospect fears or desires.
  8. Respond (as opposed to react) to the ideas—not to the person. Don't allow yourself to become irritated or insulted.
  9. Listen between the lines. Often, what is not said by the prospect is just as important as what is, or the way it is said.
  10. Use interjections.

- A few final tips for using the telephone effectively:
  1. Use a mirror to check your attitude.
  2. Be careful with the hold button. If you must put a person on hold, do so for as short a time as possible.
  3. Hang up last. No one likes the sound of the "click" in their ear.

- Prospects can be found from both conventional and unconventional sources.
  1. Physically position yourself in front of the right people.
  2. Find the orphans. They are company customers and clients that a departing salesperson left behind when leaving the company. You may adopt them.
  3. What's the itch cycle? Depending upon the product, there is an average time expectancy between purchases. In other words, a time length before one itches to buy again.
  4. Look in local newspapers. Always scour your local newspaper for prospects.
  5. Go door-to-door, business-to-business.

- Follow Sonia Cooper's motto: "Put the needs of your customers/prospects/referral sources first...and your paycheck will follow."

- Follow Sonia Cooper's six tips for winning over the gatekeepers.
  1. Treat them like they own the company. They are both the body-guard and direct link to their boss.
  2. Know them by their first name.
  3. Tell them that you need their "help."
  4. Include them in the promotional materials you pass out. Keep them in the loop.
  5. Put yourself in their shoes. How would you like to be treated in the same position?
  6. Be of service to them. Ask them if there isn't any way you can help them.
- Listen to Pat Hance's sage advice: "Continually keep your name in front of the public."
- Follow the road map, be creative at times, and most of all, always have the other person's wants and needs in the forefront of your mind.

8

Begin Your
Own Profitable
Networking Group

Here is a concept that will make you a lot of money over the long run: begin, run, and maintain your own organized networking club. You'll have to work at it. You'll have to cultivate it. The results, however, will truly pay off many times over. This is an extremely valuable way to network your way to endless referrals.

This is where you involve a diverse group of people who are either business owners or salespeople representing a certain business. You may be familiar with the concept and may possibly even have participated in a similar organization yourself. Unfortunately, however, quite often these groups are run incorrectly and do not live up to their full potential.

My mentor in this particular area is a woman from Sudbury, Massachusetts, named Tanny Mann. Tanny founded and runs a group called Sales Networks, Inc.—SNI for short. In fact, she now runs several of these groups and has attained tremendous success with them.

Tanny's organization was the first of this type in which I was involved. An excellent networker, she was a true inspiration when I began my own group after I moved to Florida several years later. I began selling for a local company and, having just relocated, had no sphere of influence to speak of to help me get started.

Tanny organized her group. She taught people how to network within the group, and she genuinely cared for the success of her members. This went a long way toward Tanny's own success. I'd like to share with you the setup and running of an organization such as Tanny's.

This chapter is based on a combination of what Tanny taught me, techniques I have learned from others, and those I've cultivated myself. The group I ran resulted in a lot of business for a lot of people, including myself. If you'll follow this advice, the group you begin, or even the group with which you are now involved, will prove to be just as successful and rewarding for you.

One Is the Magic Number

There's a limit of one person for a particular type, or category, of business: one printer, one chiropractor, one florist, one Realtor, one sign maker, one insurance person, one banker, and so on until you run out of categories. The total membership in this group can grow to be as high as you'd like, but should include just one person for each type of business so there is no competition within the group.

The intention of this networking club is to (1) develop and maintain a give-and-take relationship with as many other businesspeople as possible, (2) to train each of these people to know how to prospect for you, and (3) to know how to match you up with their 250-person sphere of influence. The intent is qualified leads, leads, leads, and more leads.

We already know how important it is in networking to give to others. It is *vitally* important to do this within your new networking club—in this case, especially, to be able to refer business to others.

Let's even give a special definition of networking as it relates specifically to this type of group. How about this: "the developing of a large and diverse group of people to and from whom you effectively and pragmatically give and get worthwhile leads." That's a mouthful, isn't it? It is also the way this group benefits everyone.

Knowing how to sell your products, goods, or services after acquiring these worthwhile leads is, of course, another very important subject. There are many excellent books on these subjects, and I hope you have either begun, or plan to begin, your own resource library. What we're talking about here, however, is simply how to get these leads and what types of leads to give.

The Different Types of Leads

In a group situation such as this, there are basically three types of leads: (1) general group leads, (2) individual leads of the "feel free to use my name" type, and (3) individual leads of the "please *don't* use my name" type.

General Group Leads

These are leads given by one member which could possibly benefit several members of the group. For example, an office building is going up along Highway 1 in Tequesta. This lead could be useful to the copier salesperson, Realtor, the insurance salesperson, the cleaning person, the sign person, and many others.

Individual Leads—Feel Free to Use My Name

These are leads given by one member to another. The lead may be a person who could use that particular service. In this case, the lead giver is friendly enough with the prospect that using the lead giver's name would be a help.

It should be made clear whether or not the prospect expects a call from the person to whom the lead was given. If that is the case, make sure you call or the lead giver will be made to look bad. That, in turn, will not result in additional leads from that person. Also, it should be made clear whether the lead is simply a lead or a presold.

A presold is where the lead giver has already established your credibility with the prospect to the nth degree and all you need to do, basically, is show up.

Individual Leads—Don't Use My Name

These are also leads given by one member to another. However, they are given with the stipulation that the lead giver's name not be mentioned to the prospect. Why not? For whatever reason, it would not be appreciated by either the prospect, or the lead giver, or both.

Possibly, that person is still a prospect for the lead giver and the lead giver might feel the prospect will resent the idea that his or her name is being given out to others.

Or the prospect could be a person who doesn't like the lead giver. That still isn't to say that person is not a good prospect. The lead giver might say, "Joe Sprazinski, I know he needs a new fax machine. Unfortunately, he and I didn't exactly hit it off, so I wouldn't use my name." Okay, so find another reason to get in there and see Mr. Sprazinski.

Important point: when lead givers don't want their name revealed to the prospect, their wishes *must be respected*. Otherwise, you'll never get a lead from that person again—or from anyone else in the group who hears that you went ahead and used the lead giver's name despite a request not to.

A Definite Agenda

Now let's turn to the procedure for these meetings. Lasting about an hour, it is a very structured type of setup and it needs to be followed to the T. If not, it will turn into just another group of people getting together and socializing, *thinking* they are networking but not accomplishing much. As the leader of the group, ensuring that the procedure is adhered to is your responsibility.

Meetings have two distinct segments: the *prenetworking* and the *formal networking* phases. Encourage members to arrive early in order to business-socialize during the prenetworking period. This helps along the "know you, like you, trust you" feelings necessary for effective networking. And it should be informal. Get as many group members as possible to know you on a personal basis.

During the formal networking phase, after calling the meeting to order, ask each person to briefly address the group, stating his or her name, company, type of product or service with which they are involved, and types of leads desired.

Here's a hint which worked very well for me when I ran my group. For your turn, develop a sort of vignette, a profile, or short commercial. You'll use that every single time, and the message will become implanted in your group members' minds and memories. Even though you might imagine it to be boring for people to hear, don't let that concern you.

You are there to do business, and as group members become more and more familiar with your word-for-word commercial, what you do will become a part of them. That is what all successful networkers strive to achieve.

Can You Relate to This?

Aren't there commercials from years ago which you can identify and still remember? "I can't believe I ate the *whole* thing" from Alka Seltzer. Two insurance commercials that come to mind are, "You're in good hands with Allstate" and "Get a piece of the Rock" (Prudential). How about this fast-food commercial: "You deserve a break today. So get up and get away." To where? Of course, McDonald's. And you know what, that particular McDonald's campaign hasn't been around for years! But you remember it, anyway, don't you?

Therefore, play your commercial over and over again, once a week, at every group meeting. Before long, what you do will be ingrained into your fellow networkers' brains. Here's an example of a short, effective commercial. If I were in real estate, I might say, "My name is Bob Burg, Realtor associate with Ocean Realty. I successfully market homes for people who wish to sell, and help those who want to buy the perfect dream home. If you hear a person mention selling a home or buying a home, that person would be a good lead for me."

That's all you need to say that week, next week, and every week in the future. As mentioned earlier, what you want to avoid is talking technical. If you're a Realtor, you wouldn't want to say, "When I list a home, first I do this, then that, then hold an open house, then this," etc. The accountant in the group would absolutely *not* talk about how to prepare a form 11-20 U.S. corporation tax return. The copy machine salesperson would not describe the bells and whistles in his product. That's not important.

You might think, "Well, the others in the group should know as much as possible about my products or service so they can help sell them." That's not so! You can sell your products or services much better than they can. You simply want them to get you the *leads*.

Here's a perfect example. There was a woman in my group who sold paper products. All kinds of paper products. Every week she would give her brief vignette, or commercial, and conclude by saying, "And remember, when you think of toilet paper, think of me."

Everyone laughed every time she said it. But I'll tell you what: when you met somebody in business who might need paper products, any type of paper products (not just toilet paper), you thought of this woman. How effective! She is a very successful salesperson. In fact, last time I spoke with her I discovered she had been promoted to sales manager of the entire company.

Your commercial should total no more than 15 or 20 seconds. Following that, thank those who gave you leads at the previous meeting or during the week. Recognition is very important, and they will appreciate the fact that you recognize them publicly. After thanking those from whom you received leads, you now give out your leads to the group and individuals.

Out Loud!!!

Please realize how important it is to state your leads publicly and enthusiastically. Do not wait until afterward and give out your leads privately. There were people in my group who feared being thought of as conceited or braggadocio for giving their leads out loud.

Why? That's just what you want to do, isn't it? If the people in the group know you're giving out leads, even to others, then they know you have the potential to get leads for them. That, of course, will make them work harder to find leads for you and will result in a "delightful cycle of success" for everyone.

As you recruit members for your group, you need to sell them on the fact that they will not necessarily receive many leads right away. Success in this group is similar to planting the seeds in an enormous garden. It takes care, commitment, diligence, and most of all, patience. Eventually, all will reap plenty.

Teach them these exact techniques. Assure them that *if* they are willing to stick with it, they will receive the rewards they desire: lots and lots of qualified leads and the foundation of a terrific network.

They must *not* miss these meetings, except in an emergency. They must schedule the meeting as a business appointment each and every week. There were people in my group who quit after two sessions because they "didn't get business from the group."

Well, they hadn't given anyone a chance to get to know them, like them, or trust them. Even then, the timing might not have been quite right. Joining a networking group won't necessarily result in instant gratification. Some people will not be willing to accept that fact and will, therefore, quit.

But another member named Tom, who sold a fairly high-ticket item, patiently cultivated the group for over a year. He received some leads, but nothing substantial. All of a sudden, a transaction came through in which three different members of the group all participated. It was truly a soap opera situation, with none of them even realizing that the others were involved, and it ended up netting Tom a huge commission. To this day, and for obvious reasons, Tom is a hard-core networker. He uses the techniques and is very successful.

Other members, depending upon the types of business with which they are involved, will see business come in quicker and more steadily, especially from fellow members. People in that category would include florists and printers or others with products, goods, or services which are often in demand. Their primary focus should be to cultivate their fellow members, and earn the business of their 250-person sphere of influence as well.

Work the Spheres of Influence

Every so often, I'm asked to observe a networking group and critique its operation. Almost without exception, the first thing I suggest is, "Stop having selling your products and services to each other as a primary goal." Instead, make it your main objective to have the group members serve as your walking ambassadors to their 250-person sphere of influence.

When recruiting or allowing members to join your group, make sure to have them checked out for honesty and integrity. If possible, recruit them by networking with others, including those in your group. Urge your members to invite prospective members—as long as it's in a business category that is presently vacant. The chances are always better that a newcomer referred by a group member will fit the profile of honesty and integrity. You don't want to give a good lead to a bad apple. That won't make you or the other members of the group look good.

In order to get the group off the ground, you may have to do some "babysitting." In other words, you need to call the members the night before the meeting to make sure they're coming. And make sure you hold the meetings early in the morning, before the regular workday begins. Sure, it can be tough getting people to wake up a little earlier one morning per week, but you know what's even tougher? Trying to get people to attend immediately after the regular workday ends. That's a battle royal!

People are normally fresher and have clearer heads in the morning. Besides, if they're motivated enough (which are the type of people you want to network with anyway), they'll get themselves up a little earlier in order to make this very important meeting. And hopefully, when their workday begins, they will get the opportunity to use the leads just received from the morning's meeting while those leads are still fresh in their mind.

To Charge or Not to Charge

People ask if they should charge a fee or dues for belonging to the group. Here's what I've experienced. At first, you won't get a lot of people willing to shell out money—not until they see the value of belonging to the group. In fact, at first, it will cost you some out-of-pocket money in time, stationery, and stamps. Be prepared to absorb those expenses in the beginning. In the long run, you know you're going to come out ahead.

Once you get the group off the ground and it has proven effective, then you can begin charging a token sum. This will pay for any miscellaneous expenses that were initially coming out of your own pocket. I charged a couple of dollars per meeting and had the manager of the host restaurant agree to have a light breakfast served. In fact, he joined our group as the caterer.

I feel it's better to start a group of your own than to join and simply be a member of another one. When it's your group, your baby, your brainchild, you have an even higher personal stake in it. You have a vested interest in making it successful. And you're positioned much stronger within the group. The other members will always have you and your products or services on their mind whenever there is a good prospect out there—and, of course, vice versa.

By the way, if you'd rather not put the effort into beginning your own group, there are plenty of groups already out there which you could join. Although the group's specific agenda may be different from what I've described, the basics are still the same. Simply use the techniques you've learned in order to cultivate relationships with these people. Most cities and towns now have several of these groups, so ask around and you'll find one. Just hope there is still an opening for your business category.

There are people such as Tanny Mann, whom I mentioned earlier, running similar groups. Like Tanny, many even run several groups as their full-time job. They charge good money to belong, but the benefits of membership are well worth it. Believe me, they work extremely hard to make it worthwhile for their members. I wouldn't want to try doing it on that level.

For most of us, these groups are simply a very effective way to build our network. Without doing it full time, you and I would be hard-pressed trying to make the group a profit center in itself. Of course, that's not our objective anyway. We're there to help each other in our own individual businesses.

Types of Categories

Regarding the actual membership, you can probably come up with a diverse group of business classifications by yourself. Here are some suggestions:

accountant, advertising representative, appliance dealer, attorney, audiovideo production person, automobile dealer, banker, boat salesperson, builder, carpet cleaner, caterer, cellular telephone salesperson, chiropractor, cleaning company, coffee service, computer salesperson, copy machine salesperson, dating service, courier service, dentist, electrician, employment agency, exercise equipment representative, financial planner, florist, funeral director, hair stylist, health club, hot tub salesperson, hotelier, insurance agent, interior designer, jeweler, landscaper, limousine service, massage therapist, moving company, nursing service, office supply representative, pager salesperson, painter, paper products person, party planning service, paving company, pest control representative, photographer, physician, podiatrist, plumber, printer,

Realtor, restauranteur, restaurant supplier, roofer, satellite dish salesperson, secretarial service, solar energy salesperson, sporting goods
store, storm windows salesperson, swimming pool sales representative,
telemarketing service, business telephone systems representative, title
company, travel agent, uniform supply service, valet service representative, veterinarian, wallpaper store representative, water cooler salesperson, water purification person, waterbed salesperson, wedding supplier,
weight loss center, window tinter...the list goes on and on.

By using your imagination, talking with others, and reading through
the Yellow Pages, you'll come up with many more business classifications or categories. I made up a list and that was only about a quarter
of it.

Often, where it seems as though two people would be in competition with one another (which you don't want), you can find a way to
make them complementary. For instance, there might be two insurance agents. However, one sells life; the other property and casualty.
That happened in the group I ran. The two referred so much business
to each other, they ended up going into business as partners.

There are also subcategories which really offer no competition. This
could include a commercial Realtor and a residential Realtor.
Depending upon how big and powerful you wish your group to
become, you can start small and work your way up to big.

What about Those Who Have Trouble Speaking in Public?

If you or someone in your group has a fear of standing up in front of
the group and speaking, realize that he or she is not alone. Public
speaking is considered by many to be their greatest fear. That's understandable. However, that's another good reason to use the same commercial every time. You'll certainly begin to feel comfortable with it,
and thus better able to speak before a large gathering.

Beyond that, I'm going to suggest you first visit as a guest, and then
enroll in an organization called Toastmasters International. There are
local chapters all over the world. Your local chamber of commerce can
direct you to a chapter near you.

Toastmasters is an organization of people dedicated to helping you
become a better speaker. And, in turn, you eventually do the same for
them. It's a very comfortable, win-win situation, and lots of fun. For
more information, you can also call their headquarters in Mission
Viejo, California, at 714-858-8255.

I've got to confess that, although I speak for a living and am a former radio and television news anchor, I still get that lousy, nervous feeling every time before I present to an audience. Believe me, you're not alone.

Other Important Points

I want to reiterate a point mentioned earlier. Sit next to different people at every meeting. Even in the formal setting you will still get the opportunity to exchange positive words and ideas with someone new, as well as establish rapport. This is a key. Remember, you want these people to know you, like you, and trust you.

Although you will see the same people every week, the little things still count. Send them articles of interest and extend the extra courtesies you offer for your other networking prospects. You can, and definitely should, mail them personalized thank-you postcards for leads. Everyone likes to be recognized, and they will continue to work hard for you if they know that recognition can be expected. Their next lead might be a great one.

Don't be afraid to toot your own horn. Always give your leads publicly. Make sure everyone knows you are working hard to help *their* business grow. That way, they will want to help *your* business grow. And everyone comes out a winner!

Key Points

- When organizing your own networking group, there's a limit of one person for a particular type, or category, of business. Thus, there is no competition within the group.
- Meetings are held one morning per week. Every week!
- The intent of the group is qualified leads, leads, leads, and more leads.
- There are three different types of leads
  1. General group leads
  2. Individual leads: "Feel free to use my name"
  3. Individual leads: "Don't use my name"
- There is a specific structured setup for the meetings.
  1. *Prenetworking.* Members arrive early to business-socialize.

2. *Formal networking.* Each member individually stands up to address the group. Develop a vignette, or short commercial, and use it every time.

- State leads and thank you's out loud.

- Concentrate not on getting these peoples' direct business but that of their 250-person sphere of influence. Cultivate them as you would anyone else in your network (thank-you notes, etc.).

9

Position Yourself as the Expert (and Only Logical Resource) in Your Field

When I say the word "astronomer," who immediately comes to mind? Most people will not hesitate even a moment before answering "Carl Sagan."

When talking about science fiction, and especially robots, what author's name might jump right out at us? Many would name the late Isaac Asimov.

What about child psychologists? Benjamin Spock. How about Vulcans? Well...Mr. Spock. Motivational speakers? Zig Ziglar, Dr. Denis Waitley, Anthony Robbins, and a few others might immediately come to mind.

What about your line of work? Who stands out in the public eye as the person your community would immediately think of? Is that person *you*? Are you so well positioned in your community that when people either need the products or services you provide or know somebody who does, they think of you—and only you? If they don't at present, they will! That is your goal.

Fellow speaker and author Peter Johnson is a marketing strategist for major corporations and organizations all over the world. A renowned genius in his field, he refers to this concept as "the science of strategic positioning." In his series, *Johnson on Strategic Marketing,* he describes it this way:

> To definitively establish in precise terms the strategic identity, image, and reputation of your specific company, your products, and your services such that in the mind of your targeted market-place there could be no acceptable alternative available any-where...regardless of price.

That definition certainly works for me. When *I* talk about position-ing oneself as the "expert" in relation to networking, however, I'm talking on a much smaller scale—an individual basis. In this case we're talking about positioning the individual as well as (actually, more than) the product or service itself. People need to make an asso-ciation in their minds between who you are and what you do for a liv-ing. After all, they know, like, and trust you. They want to help you succeed and find new business.

Act As If...and You Will Be

In this chapter, I'd like to share with you my ideas on how to attain the position of "expert" and only logical resource in your field. There are several tangible methods, but first you must put yourself in the mind frame of already being there. Imagine you are the person who has already attained success using the techniques we are going to discuss. People now come to you for information, referrals, and advice. You have already begun to use these methods and techniques for your positioning benefit, and it hasn't cost you a dime.

Positioning through the Media

One excellent way of positioning yourself as the expert is to write arti-cles for local, state, and national print media. Let's imagine you're a financial planner and you "help people create and manage wealth." I'm using that profession as an example, but you need to gear this advice toward your own particular field and find a way to make it applicable. Writing articles is a very effective way to position yourself with hundreds or even thousands of people. People automatically regard you as an authority.

Write a weekly column for your local newspaper and position your-self as the expert in your field. It must serve the public interest, so find an angle that will be welcomed by the editor of the newspaper. A consumer advocate is one possibility. Maybe you can share interesting tidbits not known by the average reader. That way people will feel they can rely on you instead of others in your field. For instance, what do you know that the public needs or wants to know about? How about the kind of investment products one should consider? What sort of products should one either be wary of or stay away from altogether? How does one protect one's assets and increase one's wealth without taking potentially catastrophic financial risks (or at least keeping those risks to a minimum)?

A chiropractor could write a weekly column on health and exercise. An accountant could write a column entitled "Tax Tip of the Week." An office products salesperson could give out suggestions regarding how to get the best quality at the lowest price. And so on and so on.

There are many, many topics that financial planners, chiropractors, accountants, office products salespeople, and practically every other person selling a product or service could use to write articles. You can, too, regardless of your profession! Just put your mind to it, and even brainstorm with your family and those in your network.

When writing this article, please keep in mind, it cannot be written as a personal advertisement. It must be kept very public interest–oriented. What you want is a byline, as well as your picture and some information about you (space permitting). You are not using this column directly as a sales tool; instead, you are using it as a positioning tool which will *eventually* turn into a sales and marketing tool. We'll talk more about that after we answer this question...

How Easy Is This to Accomplish?

The challenge you will most likely come up against is this: the editor of the newspaper will probably say something like, "But we've never done this before!" Well, you have to find a way of selling that person on why he or she should do it now.

My friend, author, and former newspaper editor Dean Shapiro also points out some very legitimate reasons why editors are not easily swayed into granting this type of situation. According to Dean, "Newspaper columns about businesses are not an easy thing for an editor to give away. They are *never* free, even when the columnist is not getting any money for doing them. *Someone* is paying for that space, and that's usually the newspaper. If the person writing the column isn't taking out a commensurate amount of paid advertising in the paper, most editors are loathe to give them 'free advertising' even when the column isn't a direct appeal for business. Just putting someone's name out there in connection with what they do is a form of advertising for them. Newspapers need ads to survive and they hate giving *anything* away gratis."

Dean continues: "Editors also have to guard against setting precedents that can come back to haunt them. Give a column to a Realtor each week and you leave yourself wide open to a chiropractor calling and saying, `Hey, you're giving Larry Soandso a column. How about giving me one? I serve more people than he does.' And then the water purification system saleswoman calls and says, `Hey, you're giving a column to a real estate broker and a chiropractor. How about one for me?' You begin to get the picture."

Dean concludes with the strongest point of all, and that is the fact that if a newspaper does give column space away, there has to be a potential tangible gain, such as an increase in paid readership resulting from that column's publication.

So you need to educate the editor on how your column is going to benefit the newspaper, the reader, *and the editor*. Remember, people naturally want to create less work for themselves, and editors are no exception. Therefore, if you can provide them with an article every week at no cost which will increase readership and help them fill a news hole with a valuable public service, they may jump at it. But be prepared for some resistance. Find a way to accomplish your goal, and you'll find the rewards worth the effort.

The $14 Million Woman

One such example is my friend and fellow speaker, Terri Murphy. Aside from being an up-and-coming professional speaker, she is a Realtor—a very successful one. I refer to Terri as "The $14 Million Woman." That's how much real estate Terri sells every year, good market or bad. One of Terri's most powerful positioning tools is her newspaper column, "Murphy on Real Estate."

She had to work for it! According to "Murph," it took her 6 months to convince the editor of her local newspaper to run her column. She says she encountered *lots* of resistance and really had to be imaginative. What Terri did was first write sample articles.

She also offered her column for free until she could prove its worth. Then she pointed out why the paper's use of syndicated columns that applied to major U.S. cities wasn't necessarily in the best interests of those living in her small town.

Terri suggested that the stories needed a local flavor, and that she was just the one to give it to them. With the combination of Terri's determination, sales ability, and logic, her column was accepted.

Eventually, "Murphy on Real Estate" went on to become syndicated in 26 newspapers nationwide.

But she didn't stop there. Terri then worked her way in as the host of a weekly radio show. She accomplished this by first sending in someone from her personal network who had connections at the station. She combined the power of her network with the authoritative positioning she already had established as a newspaper columnist.

Yes, she had to work at that one too, but of course, she managed to come through. Terri found a way to succeed. And her sales production continues to soar, in a real estate climate most people feel is cyclical.

The last time I spoke with Terri, she was in the midst of putting together a local cable television show. If her track record is any indication, there is no doubt in my mind it will be as successful as all of her other accomplishments in the media.

Forget about Exposure—It's the Positioning You're After

Once upon a time in the United States, before there was the intense competition we now face, *exposure* was all anyone ever really needed. You remember the days when it was profitable to simply hang out your shingle? People would see your sign, be *exposed* to it, and voilà! Business!

And if you or your business ever somehow managed to get mentioned in the newspaper or on television, that was it! People called you. People came to see you. You got great exposure, and that directly resulted in business.

It's a different ball game nowadays. Practically more direct salespeople, insurance agents, Realtors, lawyers, accountants, dentists, chiropractors, and multilevel marketing people are seeking customers, clients, or patients than there are people who can possibly use their services. That's why it is now so important to separate yourself from all the others and be positioned as the expert and "only resource" of whatever it is you do.

Let's get back to our newspaper column. The exposure you achieve from writing that column probably won't bring you enough business to justify the time and effort needed to get and maintain it in the first place. However, you can sure use that column as a very effective positioning tool.

Reprints from your column should be sent on a regular basis to those in your network. In your personal brochure or sales presentation kit, you should highlight the fact that *you* are the columnist on that subject for your local newspaper. Why? What's the point?

It's tremendous positioning! Aren't you successfully implying, without actually saying, that you are the *expert*. You *must* be an expert—why else would the local newspaper choose you to share your knowledge above all of your competitors? That's what Terri does, as well as many others who know the importance of what she calls "power positioning."

Let me ask you a question. Do you think Terri ever tries to get direct listings or sales from her articles and radio talk shows? Absolutely not. That would be both unethical and nonproductive. She simply positions herself as the expert by giving out worthwhile, helpful, sound advice, and it comes back to her over and over again.

What If You Still Can't Get a Column?

Sometimes, entering through the front door is so difficult that walking through the back door simply makes more sense. While waiting for the break that will land you the actual column, Dean Shapiro has some suggestions that make sense.

"Aim a bit lower and shoot for monthly or periodic articles. Submit what are known as 'filler' copy that can fill a given amount of space in a news hole when the need arises. Make sure the articles are not tied to a specific time frame, however, because they may run weeks or even months from the time they are submitted." Dean advises sending a note with your submission saying, "Please run as space permits" or something similar.

Editors, especially at weeklies, pick up on these things, usually in the last few minutes before press run when they have a 13-inch (or whatever size) hole to fill and your column, which fits perfectly, just happens to be close by in the filler file. Be sure and submit a number of them at varying lengths so the editor can have a choice to fill whatever size hole exists in those last-minute press deadline crunches.

Another technique is to "feed" story ideas to an editor. According to Dean, "Very politely (and *not* too frequently) call or write to the editor suggesting a story or stories in your field and make certain these story ideas are broad-based enough to have a wide appeal to readers. Naturally, you, as the story originator, will be quoted in it as the 'authority' and that gives it advantageous positioning strength. Eventually, you could establish yourself as the one (or at least the first) person an editor or reporter calls when a story breaks in that field. That can eventually lead to the granting of column privileges, and for now, excellent positioning."

The fact is, most people, including myself, don't know a whole lot about a lot of different things. I know nothing about financial planning. When you consider the number of financial planners who approach me to invest my money with them, and my level of ignorance, it's a scary situation. All things being equal, don't you think I want an *expert* taking care of my hard-earned money?

I also don't know much about computers, real estate, insurance, automobiles, and most other things in life. Just because salespeople in these arenas are my clients doesn't mean I have actual product knowledge. Far from it. When they know *their* products and use *my* networking techniques, or ones that are similar, that's when they become top producers.

The Truth Is *Not* Necessarily What It Appears to Be

Unfortunately, there are many people who don't have enough product knowledge to actually help their customers and clients (and many who don't care to), yet they know how to position themselves well enough to be perceived as the expert in their field.

In his book, *Direct Mail Copy That Sells,* author and renowned copywriting legend Herschell Gordon Lewis refers to the word, "verisimilitude," meaning "having the appearance of truth." Not necessarily *the truth,* but simply the *appearance* of such. Whether something is actually true, or just seems to be so, people buy what they *perceive* to be the truth. Thus, we could say, "The truth is what the truth appears to be."

Actually, I hope you disagree with my last sentence. The truth *isn't* just what it appears to be. The truth is the truth. Unfortunately, the sentence preceding that one is accurate. In fact, the reason that con artists can fool so many people is that they are experts at making them perceive what they say as being the truth.

I'm sure we can all think of a particular person or persons where this comes to mind. I'm thinking of one speaker in particular who is an absolute expert at back-of-the-room product sales. Unfortunately, unlike most speakers I have the pleasure of knowing who are wonderful, honest people, this person is not. He *is* slick, however. By the time he gets through conning his audience, they are literally racing to the product table to buy his tapes.

His program is basically one big, cleverly disguised commercial, void of any content whatsoever. His pitch (I hate that word, but it fits in this case) is so believable that every time I hear it, I almost want to buy his tapes myself. I did once, and they were next to worthless.

But I must say, he is believable. The word "verisimilitude" seems to have been made just for him. And there are others like him. Although it can be frustrating, remember—good guys (and women) *do* finish first. Sometimes it just takes a little while longer to get there. Once there, however, we stay there forever, while the con artist is always looking for a new territory because "Everybody in mine knows me."

The point is this: I know that you, the reader, know your product. You are extremely honest and trustworthy, and will use these techniques for the good of the customers and clients you serve. With that in mind, these techniques will help you position yourself as the expert, the authority in your field.

Another way you can accomplish this goal is to write for your state and national media. Again, citing real estate sales as an example, here's how. Your state board or Association of Realtors® probably has a magazine you can write for, as does the National Association of Realtors®, and other trade magazines within that field. Terri Murphy uses these media as well.

You might wonder what good does that do if other Realtors are the only ones reading it? That may be true, but in your listing and selling presentations it builds credibility with your prospects or customers if they know that you are a published author. You are perceived by your prospects as an expert (which you are). They know that even those in your profession recognize you as an authority; otherwise your article would not have appeared in their magazine.

As a Realtor, Terri also positions herself as an expert to others in her field. Consequently, she receives referrals from her peers all over North America regarding helping newcomers to her area find a place to live.

Now bear in mind that you don't have to be in any of the professions mentioned to write a column or individual articles and position yourself as an expert through their publication. Just as there are always ways to create a market for your product or service, there are ways to create a market for your articles. It is great positioning! I've personally had several hundred articles published in trade and professional magazines, and my efforts have paid off many times over.

Often, these articles are picked up and rerun by other magazines, which increases my positioning even further. Several magazines have asked me to contribute additional articles after running my first one. I get paid for some of them, but most of the time I'm only doing it for positioning.

How to Get Published

When you decide you want to write an article for a trade magazine, simply call and ask for the editor in charge of outside contributing articles or freelance submissions. Tell her your idea as concisely as possible and see if it's a match. If she thinks it is, she'll ask you to submit something, usually a query letter describing what you plan to cover in the article. Sometimes, editors will request the article itself.

I wouldn't submit anything at that point, however. Instead, ask for a set of author's guidelines and a back issue or two of the magazine. You want to see how articles are written, the average length of the articles the journal runs, the slant of the magazine, and, what kind of biography you will be given at the conclusion of the article. Then you tailor your article accordingly.

What you can do if you aim to be published in many periodicals is come up with a couple of generic articles that give good, worthwhile advice and simply gear them to a specific industry or audience and spell out what you're trying to accomplish in your article. You can consult the *Reader's Guide to Periodical Literature* or other reference books in your local library for the names of prospective magazines, or you can look through the racks at the magazines they order. Reference librarians are usually good sources of information on which publications might suit your needs. Don't be afraid to ask them; that's what they're there for.

And whenever you are published, send a press release to your local newspaper letting them know about it. If you're a chiropractor and had an article published in a chiropractic magazine, make sure the editor of your local newspaper knows that. If the local paper prints the release you send or mentions it in some other context such as a "People" column, it's another trophy you can use in order to position yourself as your community's chiropractic authority. A framed copy of a printed article hanging prominently in a waiting room is certainly an effective positioning device to those who are already patients. They can then be referring those in their sphere of influence to a recognized authority in his or her field.

You Can Also Position Yourself through the Electronic Media

Another means of positioning yourself in the community is to appear as a guest expert on local radio and television talk shows. When you call the station, don't ask to speak with the host: ask to speak to the producer. In fact, in a larger market it will probably be a segment producer. Explain to him or her what might be the advantages of having *you* as a guest on the program as opposed to others in the same field. You have to be concise and convincing because producers often get dozens of similar requests every week. You should be prepared with an angle or a hook that will snag the listeners' or viewers' attention.

If you are a medical doctor, for example, you can point out on a radio or television talk show certain practices by many in the medical profession that aren't necessarily ethical. Or you can describe a procedure that doctors should not be doing, even though many of them are. What does the public have the right to know that they're not being told?

I'm not saying you have to engage in yellow journalism or sensationalism, and I'm not suggesting that you need to use those precise examples. What I *am* saying is to "create a reason" why what you have to say is of interest to the show producers and audiences. They want a hook, an "angle." Pretend you are fishing and give them bait they'll bite on.

Remember, make the program match the audience. If you're an accountant, then appearing on a program geared toward teenagers isn't going to do you much good. You'll get exposure, but since your target audience is not watching, you won't increase your positioning. You only need people seeing you who are prospective customers, clients, or, more importantly, sources of referrals.

An excellent manual entitled *How To Get Famous* was authored by Ross Shafer of Woodland Hills, California, a well-known talk show producer, host, and stand-up comic. In this manual, not only does Ross share information on how to get on radio and television talk shows; he also talks about what to do and what not to do once you get there.

Fellow speaker and author Judith Briles of Denver, Colorado, is one of the National Speakers Association's main authorities on, as she calls it, "mastering the media." Judith, who speaks mainly on women's issues, has appeared on all the biggies including *Donahue, Oprah, Sally Jesse Raphael,* and *Geraldo.* She has used the media simply as a vehicle to position herself as an expert to her prospects, and it's worked.

Charles Garcia, a Realtor based in San Francisco, did a superb job of exploiting the media as a positioning tool. He let the segment producers of the local CBS affiliate know he was available for real estate advice and opinion. They eventually took him up on his *kind* offer.

Remember the San Francisco earthquake in 1989? A couple of days after that event a friend of Charles Garcia asked him how he thought this disaster would affect local real estate values. Charles immediately realized that a lot of San Francisco and Bay Area people were wondering the same thing.

He called the station and provided a list of topics relating to the earthquake, its effect on real estate values in different neighborhoods, and projections of what might be expected. He suggested that they wait 7 to 10 days before doing this story in order to give the market a little time to respond.

Meanwhile, Charles began doing his homework. He canvassed his colleagues in the real estate community, interviewing the managers of the major real estate offices in San Francisco and the Bay Area and consumers. He put together an interesting story on the effects of the earthquake on real estate values in the Bay Area.

In this 2-minute segment, he revealed some surprising statistics: very few real estate companies reflected a sharp increase in the number of deals falling out of escrow in the short time after the quake. Most buyers who had been in the process of house hunting before the earthquake were still looking. According to Charles, "Is the home seismically upgraded?" became the question of the day. Charles's status as "real estate expert" was reinforced.

These days Charles's brochure and mailing pieces feature a wonderful picture of him being interviewed by the two anchors. Doesn't that tell his prospects they have the opportunity to work with an expert? And when he sends this to his current customers and clients, they are proud to refer their real estate expert to their own sphere of influence.

As a footnote to this story, the first time Charles appeared on that news program was because the prior Realtor they had been using stood them up. She simply didn't show. The producers then let Charles know they were looking for a dependable real estate agent with whom they could form and develop a relationship.

Still another Realtor, Jim Boyce of Toronto, Ontario, has taken a slightly different tack. A former tennis star, he's now published in a Province tennis magazine in which he gives tennis advice, while highlighting the fact that he is a Realtor. He has also managed to acquire free advertising space in lieu of payment.

Why am I highlighting Realtors as the only examples of people using these techniques in order to effectively and profitably position themselves? Because they seem to be the ones doing it most frequently. But that doesn't mean other professions aren't doing it as well. (In fact, I'd like to hear from those of you in other professions who are also taking advantage of this unique opportunity.)

Are You an Information Resource for Others?

Let's discuss another aspect of positioning yourself as the expert: being an "information resource" for others. In other words, helping people in your community find products, goods, services, or even jobs.

You want to be that person others call to ask, "Hey, do you know a good printer?" Do you know a painless dentist? Do you know who has a good cellular phone and provides excellent service? Be that person who's almost *brokering* the information. Not for a fee, but for positioning.

On one occasion, the editor of a magazine to which I sometimes contribute articles called and asked me if I knew anybody else who could write articles on specific topics for them. Months earlier, I had suggested he use the talents of a fellow member of the National Speakers Association. He did, and that person wrote an excellent article.

When the editor called to ask for more referrals, I decided this was a good opportunity for a lot of win-win situations and excellent positioning for, and with, my other speaker friends. Not to mention the editor himself, who has a lot of pull within the association represented by his magazine.

So I contacted all the speakers within my personal network who I knew could write good articles and relayed the situation to them. By the time I contacted the editor, just a short while later, he had already been deluged with calls from my speaker friends. He loved it because his magazine was in need of a bunch of excellent articles.

That is win-win networking all around. I positioned myself with both my network of speakers *and* with the editor's network. In fact, he came right out and said, "Please let me know if there's *anything* I can do for you."

This type of positioning is actually quite easy to accomplish. Whenever you hear of someone needing something, come right out and match her up with someone who can help her. Do this consistently, and in time, people will know that you are the one to approach for this type of service.

Are You a Referral Source for Others?

When it comes to positioning oneself as a referral source, John Kuczek, president of Kuczek and Associates of Youngstown, Ohio, really has the right idea. He discovered early in his career that positioning yourself as the Big Person on Campus by way of helping others is the key to success, and he continues that practice to this day.

Addressing members of the Million Dollar Round Table at their 1991 annual meeting in New Orleans, Louisiana, Kuczek shared many of his excellent techniques with his fellow insurance sales professionals. Here's one.

According to Kuczek, "I help clients set up loans and mortgages, and they feel indebted to me because they usually dislike dealing with bankers and I help them get what they want. I also advise them on how to handle their earnings and divert some money into savings and remind them never to invest money they can't afford to lose.

"By helping clients structure mortgages and loans," continues Kuczek, "I also build a positive relationship with local banks. When I deal with people growing financially, somebody's always borrowing money. As they pay off loans, new projects come up and they are borrowing money again.

"Over the years," he adds, "I have done more and more business with bankers. By learning to use bankers, I created the ideal situation. The bankers would come to me instead of me approaching them. In the last year or so, banks have come to me and asked for referrals. I gladly oblige as long as my clients who are banking with them are getting the best service available, and that includes getting preferred interest rates on loans.

"Now that my company is comfortably *positioned* with area bankers we also ask *them* for referrals. We ask them to take a look at their customers who have commercial loans and see if they would benefit from our services. Interestingly enough, since we have begun to take this approach, we have actually had situations where banks are now calling us to refer clients. Banks are an indispensable part of my business."

Did you notice the phrase he used? "Comfortably positioned" with bankers. He's a man who knows the meaning of long-term business relationships, which is what networking is all about. No wonder John Kuczek is a qualifying member of the Million Dollar Round Table, Top of the Table, and Forum, which are some of the highest honors one can be awarded as a member of the National Association of Life Underwriters.

Positioning Through the Law of Large Numbers

Even if many of your prospects are currently doing business with your competition, if you feel they are worth your persistence, stay with them. With your excellent, classy follow-up, you'll be ready to step in if your competitor messes up, moves on, or for some other reason loses that person's account and referrals.

In his book, *Swim with the Sharks without Being Eaten Alive,* author Harvey Mackay points out that you should position yourself as the number two person to every prospect on your list and keep adding to that list. He continues that if your list is long enough, there are going to be number ones that retire or lose their territories for a hundred other reasons and succumb to the Law of Large Numbers.

According to Mackay, "If you're standing second in line, in enough lines, sooner or later you're going to move up to number one." I agree totally. Totally! Especially, if you're doing enough things right, such as using the follow-up techniques I've been describing in this book.

Again, if you're the number two person on enough lists, and you're doing the right things, you'll eventually *have* to move up to number one on many of those prospects' lists. And in the networking sense, of course, that doesn't mean being number one just for that person's direct business but for his or her referrals as well.

An excellent analogy has to do with one of my niche markets, the insurance industry. In that profession actuaries are wizards with numbers who can actually predict, almost to the percentage point, how many people in a given area are going to die as a result of traffic fatalities over a certain holiday weekend. Morbid, but true. The only thing they can't tell you is *who* they will be.

Mr. Mackay points out that the insurance industry has basically been built on the Law of Large Numbers. That's why, as Mackay says, if you position yourself as the number two person on enough lists, then sooner or later you've got to work your way up to number one on many of those lists.

What If They Are Already Someone's Customers?

What if many of your networking prospects are currently doing direct business with someone else. Do you realize that you can still get their referrals? Yes, even if you are number two on their list for direct business, you can be number one for their referrals. And position yourself to eventually get their direct business while you're at it.

You may be wondering, "Why would a person possibly refer business to *me* if they're doing business with someone else?" Numerous reasons. All things being equal, they may be doing business directly with your competitor out of a sense of loyalty to that person or maybe even to somebody else—a friend or family member. How many times have you been told by prospects that they *have* to do business with someone because they are somehow connected or related? It's happened to most of us.

If you've impressed this person enough, however, she'll go out of her way to get you referral business. One networking prospect felt so bad that his wife gave some business to a competitor that he actually went on a hunt to find some referrals for me. He was quite successful in that particular venture. Therefore, so was I.

I had earned his loyalty and help by going out of my way for him previously, using my network to assist him with information he needed to help some of his clients. What goes around *does* come around.

So are your networking prospects worth your persistence? If so, stay with them. Position yourself as the number two person on a prospect's direct business list, if that's all the current situation will allow. Position yourself as number one, however, for their referrals. Eventually you may be number one for *both*.

Using the skills and techniques described in this chapter, you will become positioned as the expert, and only logical resource, in your field.

The King of "Positioning" Books

One book I highly recommend for those interested in truly mastering the technique of positioning (yourself and your business) is entitled, *Positioning: The Battle for Your Mind* (Warner). Authored by advertising mavens and marketing strategists Al Ries and Jack Trout, this book is an absolute gold mine of positioning strategies. Although written from the perspective of an ad person, you will find the authors' techniques and strategies totally applicable to the goals you are trying to accomplish.

Key Points

- Act as if you are already powerfully positioned.
- Position yourself (for free) through the media.
  1. Write columns and articles for local, state, and national print media. These must be consumer-oriented.
  2. Prove to the editor why your information is important for his or her readership.
- Exposure alone is no longer a money maker. Positioning yourself as the expert in your field is the key.
- Verisimilitude is having the appearance of truth.
- Being a guest or resource for television and radio interviews is another excellent positioning tool. You must have a hook or angle that will make you a desirable guest in the producer's mind.
- Be an information resource (jobs, services, etc.) for those in your network.
- Position yourself through the Law of Large Numbers.

10

Customer Service: The Networker's Best Friend

"If you invent a better mousetrap, you can sit back and wait because the world will beat a path to your door." No doubt you've heard that saying. Well, the day of the "better mousetrap" is over, I'm afraid.

You can build the very best mousetrap in the world. You can network yourself and your product to the point where referrals are coming in faster than you can count them. But if you don't provide excellent customer service after establishing a niche in the marketplace, a path *will* be beaten to your door—but by bill collectors, not by customers.

More than ever, we have to earn people's repeat business and referrals by providing the best customer service we possibly can. Nothing will make your newly developed network crumble faster than a stale cookie than not providing proper caring and service.

The Big Eight

I'd like to share with you my eight basic rules of customer service as they relate to networking:

Every Employee Is in Sales

Even those people in your company who are not salespeople are salespeople. What I mean is this. Everyone from the CEO to the lowest person on the totem pole is selling the public every day on why they should or should not be doing business with you.

Studies have shown that each time customers have a positive experience with you or your place of business, they will tell 4 other people. On the other hand, any time they have a negative experience, they'll tell 11 people. And believe me, they'll rush out to tell them! I do it myself!

A surefire way to destroy our newly developed sphere of influence is to forget that we need to *continue* selling people on us. One bad apple really *can* spoil the whole bunch.

Being a professional speaker, I'm always flying, and there's one airline I use most frequently. Practically all the flight attendants representing this airline are absolutely wonderful people, making their passengers feel *great* about flying with them.

But once I had a negative experience—a flight attendant who really was quite nasty. To this day, when I think of that airline, I still cannot help wincing at the memory of that one incident with that one flight attendant, even though it happened years ago.

Yet everyone I have encountered since the incident has been just as helpful and pleasant as the others before it. I'm still loyal to that airline because I realize that this particular flight attendant was an exception. Nonetheless, the seeds of change were planted in my mind, weren't they? Do any of us, or those in our company, ever plant the seeds of change in the minds of our customers, clients, or fellow networkers?

If You Think Your Customers Are Not King, Try Running Your Business Without Them

We need to constantly keep in mind the fact that our customers pay our salaries and commissions. If we own a business, we need to make sure our employees realize the same thing.

A restaurant in my town comes to mind. Since I love to eat, I'm always in restaurants. That's where you see both the best and worst of customer service. This place has decent food, but not the best, and their prices are very high. Nonetheless, they do a great business. They treat their customers tremendously, and it's appreciated. I know whenever I go there that I will feel welcome. They go out of their way to make me feel good. It's worth the price to feel that good.

One of my corporate clients, American Bankers Insurance Group, has a slogan: "The Customer Is the Boss." When they hire somebody or send an agent into the field representing them, that person must be what they call "Boss-oriented."

According to vice chairman Frank Baiamonte, "In our recruiting process, we are only interested in people who already bring a 'boss-oriented' mindset to our company." He adds, "At American Bankers Insurance Group, service is not a department; it's everybody's job."

Don't Ever Tell Customers They're Wrong

This rule can be best illustrated by citing a personal example. One day I had an appointment at the place where I used to get my hair cut. I came in at 1 o'clock, and the receptionist at the desk asked me what I was doing there. The conversation went something like this:

BOB: I have an appointment at 1 with Barbara.

RECEPTIONIST: No, you don't. Your appointment is at 1:30.

BOB: No, I'm sure it's at 1 o'clock. I even wrote it down, right here. (showing my appointment book)

RECEPTIONIST: You're wrong! It's at 1:30.

Well, one of three things obviously happened: either I was wrong, or she was wrong, or there was simply a misunderstanding between the two of us at the time we set the appointment.

In the meantime, however, she really offended me by telling me so emphatically that I was wrong! She insulted her customer. But since I was there already, I took my seat to wait for Barbara. The manager came over and asked, "Bob, what's wrong? You're not your usual friendly, smiley self."

I told her what had happened and that my feathers were just a bit ruffled at being told so emphatically that I was wrong. She replied, "Bob, I feel bad about that, but you have to realize, my people don't make mistakes!"

Well, the manager just made a mistake herself. In fact, she compounded the error made by her receptionist. Three months later, when Barbara left, the manager told me the salon would still like my business, claiming they could continue to serve my needs just as well. I thanked her for the offer, but the incident I just cited was still fresh in my mind.

Now what do you think I did? Did I stay there, or did I follow Barbara 6 miles down the road and out of my way? That's right, I followed Barbara. Why? For one reason, Barbara gives a pretty good haircut; for another, she doesn't tell me I'm wrong.

The owner of the largest dairy store in the world is a most famous customer service success story. For years he has run his business from the base of two rules that are *literally* etched in stone in a huge rock at the entrance to his store.

Rule No. 1:   The customer is always right.
Rule No. 2:   If the customer is ever wrong, reread Rule No. 1.

This very basic philosophy can work for each and every one of us, regardless of our profession.

Deliver What You Promise and a Little Bit More

Again, let me cite another personal example. One morning I went to breakfast at a local franchise restaurant. On the menu they had something which looked very appetizing. I don't remember exactly what it was, but it was something like "eggs with spinach, *smothered* with cream sauce." Now I *love* cream sauce, as indicated by my ever-expanding waistline, and I ordered that particular meal. When the meal was delivered to me, it looked very good. The eggs looked great, the spinach looked tremendous, but with just a *touch* of cream sauce.

I politely called the waitress over and asked, "Could I please get a little extra cream sauce?" I have to say, when I said a little extra, she really took me at my word. She brought me about a thimbleful of sauce. Since I'm really not the type who likes to complain, I ate the spinach and eggs with the little bit of cream sauce.

When she brought me the check, I noticed an extra charge of 50 cents for the cream sauce! Now I'm not cheap, but I had a definite problem with that. When I went to pay my check at the cashier stand, the manager saw me, motioned to me, and asked, "Did you enjoy the meal?" I said, "I certainly did. The eggs were great, the spinach was tremendous, but the only problem I have is that the menu said it was *smothered* with cream sauce. In fact, there was just a little on it. When I asked for more, just a little was brought over. That's okay," I continued, "but I was charged an extra 50 cents for the cream sauce, which turned out to be even less than what was promised on the menu."

With that, the manager grabbed the check out of my hand. He looked at it, looked at me, looked back at the check, and looked at me again. Then he came to his decision. He said, "Sir, I'll tell you what I'm going to do. I'm going to refund your 50 cents, but I've got to tell you, if we were to deliver everything we promised on the menu, we'd go out of business!"

Well, I don't know if they'll go out of business from doing things like that or not, but they certainly will *not* get my repeat business. Nor will they ever get the business of my sphere of influence.

On the other hand, there's the local Chevron station in my town. They call themselves a "Complete Service Station." They are, and more. Never have I experienced a service station that makes you feel as welcome as they make you feel. I wouldn't go anywhere else for gas unless I was 30 miles out of town and puttering along on an empty tank.

The local body shop owner who services my car is the same way. I'm totally ignorant when it comes to cars, and probably considered an easy mark by many mechanics. I have been taken advantage of in the past. But this guy and his crew are great with me, even letting me know when I don't need work I may have thought I needed. You can be sure I've referred a ton of business to them including, at one time or another, everyone on my staff. Jim Dees, of Jim Dees Automotive, is a good man, who delivers on what he promises and a little bit more.

Going the Extra Mile, or Even the Extra Step, Is Worth All the Paid Advertising in the World

One morning before an afternoon program I was putting on in Kansas City, Missouri, I pinched a nerve in my neck. In pain, I called the desk for some ice. Tonya, the front desk clerk, was quick to respond and had ice sent right up. Every 30 minutes after that, Tonya called my room to see if I was okay. Right before I went downstairs for my program, Tonya checked up on me, and again when I finished.

It sure was nice to know somebody cared without anything being in it for her! When I told her superiors about it, they said that was "commonplace for Tonya." I'm sure the Kansas City Marriott is very proud of her.

Another client is the Ritz Carlton. Whenever you ask people on their staff how to get to a certain location within the hotel, they don't just point you in the right direction. They stop what they're doing and escort you there! In fact, both of those incidents exemplify what my friend and fellow speaker Lou Heckler calls "the Wow factor."

Gifford Hampton, manager of the Palm Beach, Florida, branch of the Bank of Boston, told me another great story about going the extra mile.

It seems a woman who had recently moved to Palm Beach from the Midwest came to the bank to discuss the possibility of their handling her account. Before she made any final decision on where to bank, however, she had to go to Boston to visit her daughter. She was going for about 6 weeks and, being a bit elderly, needed a professional to care for her.

Unfortunately, neither her daughter nor anyone else seemed to be able to locate a person with whom they felt comfortable. Well, the

Palm Beach branch cared enough to help. Networking with a sister branch in the Boston area they searched and searched and finally found somebody, actually a husband-and-wife team, to take care of this woman.

The woman was able to enjoy her vacation with a true sense of security. When she returned to Palm Beach, she opened up an account with that branch. Doesn't it make sense? It ties right in with the saying by the great speaker and founder of the National Speakers Association, Cavett Robert: "People don't care how much you know until they know how much you care."

Your Receptionist Is One of Your Most Important Sales People

So make sure he or she is trained to do the job. I hear horror stories from many people regarding the way they are treated on the telephone. I've certainly experienced it myself—and from big, successful, important companies that you'd think would know better.

Even they can't get away with that negative treatment for too long before turning some people off, destroying the company one person (or should I say 250 people) at a time. We can't take the chance of getting away with poor customer service for a second in our own businesses.

Not that we should want to. We need to stress that those who answer the phone know how to make a person feel glad they called. They are the initial contact between our prospects, customers, clients, fellow networkers, and us.

This is what usually happens: companies take their most inexperienced person and stick them on the telephone, not realizing the importance of first impressions. There's an old saying, "You never get a second chance to make a good first impression."

I receive numerous compliments on the way my office staff handles people on the phone. Call my office sometime. They make you feel important—because you *are!*

Here is a tip I first learned from fellow speaker and telephone skills authority David Allan Yoho. When concluding a telephone conversation, let the other person hang up first. You don't want them to hear that cold "click" in their ear, because they may think you're glad to be through with them. Have you ever felt that way when someone hung up the phone just as you finished saying good-bye? That's how it feels to them as well.

Return Telephone Calls Promptly

Some people are just *too busy* to make money. Have you ever had somebody tell you he was just too busy to return your call. We never know who's calling, do we? It could be a prospect or a potential networking prospect.

When it comes to networking, we can't allow people in our network to feel we're being aloof and not responsive to their phone calls. If they feel they're second bananas and aren't on our priority list to return their calls, our network is going to dissolve right before our eyes.

When I was living up north, I was at a chamber of commerce card exchange, hosted and sponsored by a local restaurant. It had just opened and was trying to make a name in the community. The manager announced they were going to offer certificates that we could purchase as gifts for other people to come and eat at the restaurant.

Neat idea. Not long afterward, I felt I owed a networking associate an extra special thank you for some help he'd given me. Wanting to do something nice for him and his family as my way of showing my appreciation, I called the restaurant manager to purchase a $100 gift certificate.

The manager wasn't in, so I left my name and number. I told the person answering the phone that I had met the manager at the card exchange function the restaurant hosted. What I didn't say was why I called. You see, I didn't want to say that I was calling to buy something; I just wanted to call and say I was Bob Burg, to see if the manager thought that was an important enough reason to call back. Was he customer-oriented?

He had met me very briefly and maybe he didn't remember me. Or maybe he thought I was calling to *solicit business.* He never called back. I had been ready to spend $100. Well, actually, I did spend $100, but it was with another restaurant. That one called me back.

It Isn't Necessarily *What* We Say But *How* We Say It

In my business I stay at many hotels. Some are tremendous and the staff is great. Some aren't so tremendous and the staff isn't quite so great. In one particular hotel, the person at the registration desk was saying all the right things, but all the wrong way.

She referred to people as "Sir" and "Ma'am," but very coldly. Soon it was my turn to register. As I was filling in all the information she asked, "Did you fill in this line, sir?" I said, "No I..." and she very quickly interrupted. "Please fill in that line, sir," she said very harshly and coldly. She was saying "sir," but she really didn't mean it! And the customer, and those listening, could tell easily.

A Positive Example

On the other hand, my friend and fellow speaker, Glenna Salsbury, tells the story of a young English teacher who had worked hard all year long trying to help an Asian transfer student master the English language. Understandably, the student was very appreciative.

On the final day of school, the teacher walked into the classroom and on her desk was a single yellow rose. Next to it was a note written by the young man. It read, "Dear Teacher, one day this rose will fade and die, but you will *smell* forever!" Now, the words may not have been exactly right, but do you think she was insulted or complimented?

Of course, she was delighted because of the intention. Sometimes, it isn't what we say, it's how we say it! Our pets know what we mean by the way, tone, and manner we talk to them. It's safe to say our customers, clients, and networking prospects can sense the same thing.

Key Points

- It isn't enough to simply build the network. It must be maintained and advanced by superb customer service.
- There are eight rules of customer service:
    1. Remember that we are salespeople.
    2. If you think your customers are not king, try running your business without them.
    3. Don't ever tell customers they are wrong.
    4. Deliver what you promise and a little bit more.
    5. Going the extra mile, or even the extra step, is worth all the paid advertising in the world.
    6. Your receptionist is one of your most important sales people.
    7. Return telephone calls promptly.
    8. It isn't necessarily *what* we say but *how* we say it.

11
Cross-Promotions: An Interview with Jeff Slutsky

When we think of two people networking with each other, especially as its pertains to referrals, we look at the ideal situation as being, "This person finds leads for that person and that person finds leads for this person." And that, in itself, has the makings of a fine, mutually beneficial, give-and-take, win-win relationship.

Now, let's expand our horizons a bit, and imagine these two people actually going in on a joint promotional venture: two individuals jointly planning the idea and goal of a carryover business. In order to learn how to do this effectively and profitably, I sought the advice of expert Jeff Slutsky, author of the best selling book *Streetfighting: Low Cost Advertising/Promotions for Your Business.*

In this book, Jeff, a former advertising agency executive, showed retail businesses how to "outsmart, not outspend," their competition.*

We began our discussion by talking about Jeff's streetfighting concept, and then focused on cross-promotions as an extremely effective and profitable way for two networkers to dramatically increase their business with little expense.

---

*A brilliant piece of work, Jeff has been featured in media including the *Wall Street Journal, Inc.* Magazine, *USA Today, SUCCESS* Magazine, *Entrepreneur* Magazine, and on numerous radio programs and television talk shows including *The Sally Jessy Raphael Show.* The latest of his five books is called *How To Get Clients* (Warner).

BOB: What is "streetfighting"?

JEFF: Streetfighting is a descriptive term used to illustrate an attitude toward marketing, promotion, sales, pretty much outthinking the competition, not outspending. When something is considered to be streetfighting, it is usually clever, smart, and effective and done without wasting money. In the best-case scenario, it is something that substantially saves money or gets twice the value for the money. So there are two elements: Number one, it has to get results. And number two, it has to do it for less money.

BOB: Given the incredible and ever-growing competition in today's business and sales environment, how important is it for today's "on-the-street" salesperson to be able to use these streetfighting techniques to get new business without all of the added expense?

JEFF: It gets more and more important every day. Many companies and products have the same advantages and disadvantages. These include product quality, price, and the ability to pay for advertising. Streetfighters must be able to give themselves the edge by consistently being able to outsmart the competition.

BOB: What's your philosophy of building referrals from an existing client?

JEFF: Well, to increase referrals, you must increase the credibility and rapport you have with your client. If you're going to retain the relationship, it's important that you have developed rapport and cemented the relationship along the way. In other words, instead of having gone after the sale right away, you moved the relationship along at the pace best meeting the needs of that particular prospect or client.

All of that includes the first contact, the selling process, and especially after the sale, via great customer service. As you know, it costs a lot more to bring in a new client than it does to keep a current one. It's also more cost-effective to have clients who want to refer business to you.

BOB: What might be one example of a very basic cost-effective streetfighting technique?

JEFF: I'm personally a strong believer in using testimonial letters in the presentation in order to gain credibility. This is a letter in which a third party has said that I do a good job, that my company does a good job, and the product or service is good. So it isn't just my word, it's basically a referral, and it costs nothing at all to get. This is a very, very powerful sales tool. Great client relationships practically assure that you will have as many of these letters or referrals as you want when talking to a new prospect.

Taking it a step further, if you sell to different types of industries, you'll want to have testimonial letters from those specific industries. That tells the prospect you are an expert in that particular field. While many professionals and salespeople use this technique sometimes, a streetfighter uses it all the time.

Any kind of good publicity will also help greatly. After the inbound calls that, hopefully, you'll get, you can reproduce that media exposure, put it into print form, and use it as a positioning tool to increase credibility. (*Note:* This technique is covered in Chapter 11.)

Public speaking is also another tremendous opportunity to gain exposure, credibility, and the edge over your competition. Let's face it, when you do a speech for a civic club or organization and can relate it to your product or service, you have literally put yourself on a pedestal in front of your audience. This doesn't mean you have to be a professional speaker, but if you have something of value to offer to the community, a number of different avenues are open to you. A lot of organizations, for example, seek luncheon speakers, and if you present the information to these people, you are looked upon as the expert.

A good example is a cardiologist who gave seminars at retirement homes for senior citizens on the proper maintenance of their cardiovascular system—proper diet, exercise, and so on. Because of conducting these free seminars and because he took the time to meet with people, when they needed a cardiologist, or knew someone who needed a cardiologist, they went to him. This went a long way toward building up his practice.

BOB: What about a salesperson selling a generic product or service? Obviously, they can't simply do a sales presentation.

JEFF: In that case, a salesperson must gear his or her presentation to the consumer's point of view, finding a particular area with specific audience appeal and building on that appeal. How will that product or service be able to solve their particular problem? For example, retirement is always a big issue, so if you sell investments or insurance, you can show people how to retire with a million dollars while making only modest monthly contributions. You are conveying something of value without it being a commercial. You definitely don't want it to be a commercial. Given that caveat, this can be a great venue or means of letting people know what you do.

Cross-Promotions: The Ultimate in Win-Win Networking

BOB: One of the great concepts you developed in your business was the cross-promotion. This, to me, is the quintessential example of win-win networking. Before we delve into its uses by the salesperson or professional, what exactly is a cross-promotion?

JEFF: Cross-promotions have actually been around for a very long time. The oldest cross-promotion I'm aware of was done by Benjamin Franklin over 200 years ago. He ran a special certificate in *Poor Richard's Almanac*. He cross-promoted with Paul Revere, who gave a special deal on his pewter ware if the person bought *Poor Richard's Almanac*. This served to increase the value of the magazine, and the consumer could buy the pewter for 2 cents less. This cross-promotion worked out well for both gentlemen. It was like the first coupon. In my own case, when we started cross-promotions with our retail clients, we found out cross-promoting can go beyond retail sales into direct sales or just about anything.

BOB: How does a retail cross-promotion work?

JEFF: A simple cross-promotion could be nothing more than a fast-food place that is trying to gain more customers. They would set up a relationship with any other type of merchant that reaches the same type of customer base. Let's say the goal of the fast-food place is to go after children to promote their kiddie meals. So they could approach a Toys-R-Us, a kiddie shoe store, a kiddie clothing store, or a children's bookstore and set up a win-win, cross-promotion. The key is to find a cross-promotion partner that targets the type of people you want.

BOB: Let's take the example of a pizza place and a video store. Something like that would seem to go hand in hand. How would that work?

JEFF: That's a classic cross-promotion; pizza, especially if the store does delivery or carryout, and video, which is home entertainment. Both involve an activity at home, so it makes a lot of sense. if you are the owner of the pizza place, you would approach the video store owner and say, "How would you like to provide your customers with something extra—a way they can get a little bit more for their money when they come in to rent your videos, and a great way for you to personally thank them for being your customer?"

You might end up offering a certificate (I don't like to use the word coupon) for $2 off a large pizza that the video store would distribute to their customers. The actual offer is irrelevant as long as it has some sort of value, savings, or freebie attached to it. So it gives the video store an excuse to handle your advertising for you free.

So all of a sudden a person goes in and rents three videos. It costs them six or seven bucks which seems like a lot of money to them. But, "Thank you for coming in and here is something special for you. When you order your pizza from Joe's Pizza Parlor, you're going to save $3." The video store owner, in essence, is telling the customer: "You really only spent $4, not $7, with us today." The customer then goes away feeling good about doing business with the video store for having gotten something extra."

This as an example of a one-way cross-promotion. All that is required on your part is to provide the video store with certificates. Keep in mind that it's important to put the name of the cross-promotion partner right on the actual printed piece. A nice added touch is to put the video store owner or manager's name and signature—"Compliments of Dave Johnson"—on it as well. This technique works really well.

A two-way cross-promotion, on the other hand, is even easier to set up because it is, essentially, "I'll hand out yours and you hand out mine"—the ultimate networking. The difference is now you have to reciprocate. You have to go that extra mile and actually distribute. In practice, this is fine to do once in a while, but it is difficult to do regularly. When we set up cross-promotions for our clients, we do it on a weekly basis, so we're doing about 50 a year. You might just decide you don't want to hand out 50 certificates all the time. But it might be just the right approach for some really big cross-promotions.

A two-way cross-promotion has another advantage in that you don't have to have an offer on the piece itself for it to contain value. The very fact that you're doing it for them means they will hand out your advertising, and it could be nothing more than a reinforcement of another campaign or just a regular ad, but it doesn't have to be a coupon or certificate of value.

Reverse cross-promotions are totally different. Back to the example of the pizza store. Let's say the video store customers are coming into my store with the certificates to buy my pizza. You might respond with, "Thank you for coming into my store and buying pizza. As a little extra gift I've contacted five other merchants in my area: the ice cream shop, the shoe store, the video store, the car wash, and the beauty parlor. I've created a coupon booklet, and if you use all five coupons, you're going to save $20." So while the customer may have spent $10, she actually gets $20 back. For my part I have a premium of great value to give away. After all, many people often pay $20 or $30 for actual coupon books. This one they get for free just for buying from me. The result is a lot of added value to my business for the mere cost of a little bit of printing.

The other advantage of the reverse cross-promotion is that all 5 or 10 or 15 or 20 of the reverse cross-promotion participants owe me a favor, and now I can set up one-way cross-promotions with them very easily. So essentially, it's really a two-way in disguise, but I'm taking care of all of my two-way obligations in one effective little booklet or packet.

This technique is also good for doing theme cross-promotions, which might be important for a certain type of salesperson. Let's say you have a jewelry store. You want to cross-promote with several other companies which cater to weddings—something very specific. Let's say you approach a tuxedo rental place, bridal shop,

limousine service, photographer, musical band, etc. These businesses can't always reach the prospects before they make their deci-
sions on who to hire for these services. Where is the first place people go when they get engaged? They go to the jewelry store.

BOB: And all else being equal, you want them buying their wedding
rings from you, not from the jewelry store down the street.

JEFF: Exactly! So the reverse cross-promotion is, "If you buy your ring
from us, there is a $250 gift packet of great value for your wedding.
It has 20 or more certificates from the wedding cake on up. It not
only saves them money but practically plans their wedding for them.
So it's a great closing device for someone to make a decision. And
again, the promotion is at a very low cost. Reverse cross-promotion
becomes targeted by an event or by a specific type of product.

BOB: Now, this was a jewelry store owner or salesperson who set this
up. What about the other wedding suppliers who want to get in on
the ground floor of the wedding plans?

JEFF: It really doesn't matter which of these businesses you are in. If I
was the tuxedo shop, for example, I would go to the jewelry store
and try to set up the promotion. I might possibly suggest the idea
for the packet as long as I would be assured to get the business for
my tux shop. The key point is that I would try to set this up with a
lot of jewelry stores because that is where I'll get my referrals and
my leads.

So, as a cross-promoter, you pick out any kind of special event
and you figure out what else they have to buy. The neat thing
about cross-promotion is this: not only does it cost nothing, except
for a little bit of quick printing, but it is so targeted. Most advertising is untargeted except for direct mail or maybe telemarketing.
With a cross-promotion I can find my customers, if I know who
they are, and target by virtue of the cross-promotion partner I use.

I'll share with you one of the biggest success stories in cross-promotions ever. It has to do with a comic book store in Ohio. I had
just completed doing a whole series of training programs for
Marvel Comics, a big client of mine.

Well, comic book buyers are a very specialized type of audience.
Only a very small percentage of the population collects comic
books compared to mass media. It's not like eating pizza, which
appeals to almost everybody. Video rentals are fairly broad-based
as well. But comic books are still fairly specialized.

When the movie *Batman Returns* came out, which was a big, big
event, the comic book store owner set up a cross-promotion with
the manager of the movie theater that carried that movie. This
comic book store, of course, carries *Batman* comic books, *Penguin*,
and *Cat Woman* comic books, and all the other related ones.

Naturally, anyone attending that movie *might* be in the market
for comic books. But the important thing is, you know that anyone

who is into comic books is going to be at that movie. Now you have found your target market. So the cross-promotion is set up and here's what happened.

The theater employees handed out to moviegoers about 10,000 certificates for $1 off of the higher-end, more expensive *Penguin* and *Cat Woman* comic books. The comic book store owner got 150 returns out of 10,000. Although that is not a very high percentage, it doesn't matter. All that matters is the return on investment.

Out of the 150 redemptions, and this is the important part, over 100 customers became regular customers. A regular average customer, according to the owner, spends $10 a week in his store. If you apply the numbers and you've got 100 additional regular customers, that translates into $52,000 in sales the first year alone—all from that one cross-promotion.

Let's take it a step further. Most comic book stores live off referrals from friends. If those 100 new, regular customers refer their friends, then that $52,000 figure is just the beginning.

BOB: When we talk about the sphere of influence of the average person being 250 people, if they can refer just five of those people, what a success!

JEFF: You can still start with these 100 people just bringing in *one* friend apiece. Now it goes from $52,000 to $110,000 in extra income.

That certainly demonstrates the potential power of a cross-promotion when you target the cross-promotional partner appropriately. Not only is a movie theater a good target audience to network with if you have a comic book store, but it was that specific *type* of movie.

BOB: How would somebody more into direct-contact sales, such as an insurance person, Realtor, computer salesperson, or copying machine salesperson, use a cross-promotion? And what about professionals, such as accountants, lawyers, or dentists, who need to bring in new business but can't blatantly sell? How do they begin the cross-promotion process?

JEFF: Here's a good example. This woman is a pharmaceutical representative whose job is to get in front of the doctor and present her case for the drugs that she represents. That is not necessarily an easy thing to do, since there is a lot of competition out there in that particular field.

She knew that a significant percentage of the doctors that she called upon were avid golfers. Not a big surprise. So she asked herself the key question: What other businesses or organizations would also benefit from having access to those same doctors?

One thing that came to mind was one of the big discount golf franchises, and in her city there were four units. So let's say out of all the doctors she calls, 40 or 50 are avid golfers. Doctors are usually not poor, so when they spend money on golf, they probably spend a lot of money on clubs and everything else.

So I suggested that she approach the franchisee of the four stores in this area and say, "Listen, I call on a number of doctors and other golfers. If you'll give me a gift certificate that entitles them to a free sleeve of Titleist golf balls (this being a top name brand), I'll make sure to put it directly in their hands."

Keep in mind, Bob, we are talking about a retail item that is worth about $7 or $8, so it costs the franchise owner $3 or $4. What does it usually cost that retailer to get a potential customer in that front door? They probably spend $20 or $30 per person on mass media advertising to get them in for the first time.

Now here she is offering to go out there to her people and give them a gift certificate that will cost the franchisee only $4. She explained that as she handed these out, she would sign her name to authorize them and require the doctors to appear with the certificate personally to redeem it.

She also used this as an incentive to get the doctors to see her. She had to sign the certificate right in front of them and explain that they needed to take this to the golf shop personally in order to take advantage of the gift.

As far as the golf shop owner was concerned, return on investment was the key. Nobody goes in and just gets the golf balls. Golfers look at the clubs and everything else and possibly become regular customers. At the very least, the retailer gets that doctor's name on their list.

As far as our salesperson is concerned, she now has the ability to distribute, *for free*, these sleeves of Titleist golf balls, which would normally cost her $7 or $8. If she did that 50 times without company reimbursement, it would run into some money. Instead, everybody wins, the ultimate in cross-promoting and the ultimate in networking.

BOB: What is crucial is how she used the incentive to get past the gatekeeper and right in front of the doctor.

JEFF: The doctor had to physically sign it in her presence to validate it. That was one of the techniques that she used to make sure that she got to see the doctor in person. It had to carry both her signature and the doctor's signature and it had a tight expiration date. They had to redeem within 2 weeks. It was just one little thing that allowed her to get in to see the doctors a little more often.

BOB: The next step would be to find something else doctors like and set up a cross-promotion with another vendor, right? After a couple of times, the doctors associate her visit with a free gift, and they see her every time. And in her type of business, frequency is the name of the game.

JEFF: Another example is a life insurance salesperson whose specialty and niche market is helping people build for retirement. You're trying to sell what are known as 10/35 exchanges. It's an equity-to-term conversion of sorts that will benefit older people by giving them necessary cash they can live on.

You're trying to pick up new clients. For this, you could use the reverse cross-promotion approach. Let's say you find someone wanting to save for retirement. Not only are you going to help her save money, but you're going to help her save money for those things she needs for her retirement.

What is it that people need for retirement? Maybe they want membership to a golf club, or money off at a restaurant—an early-bird special anytime they want. In other words, benefits that offer special consideration. So you think it through and write down 10 or 15 of these merchants or salespeople together.

You let them know that you are a life insurance salesperson and will be calling on some very wealthy people who spend money on cars, homes, club memberships, food, and so on. You are giving these people an excellent opportunity to position themselves in front of this very lucrative market.

We are talking about the so-called silver generation, and every time I get new clients or clients that increase their coverage, I would provide them with a thank-you. This thank-you is going to be a packet which almost looks like a wedding invitation containing maybe a dozen nicely printed certificates as a thank-you from me, their agent. It will represent hundreds of dollars of savings. Not only am I helping them save money for retirement, but I'm helping them save money now and it's a nice thank-you. I could use this as a closing device.

BOB: Could you use this as a *opening* device as well? Let's face it—often the toughest part of doing business is getting that first face-to-face appointment with the prospect.

JEFF: As an opening tool, you would maybe not have as elaborate a package. It depends on whether you could get a restaurant to do a two-for-one, which could run into some money for them. In some cases you can get them to do freebies. Or you could offer gift certificates that are worth $25: $5 at this restaurant and $5 at this place. The restaurant owners will do that in a second just for the introduction to those people.

You can use this to get in front of somebody. You can use it as a closing tool. You can use it as a frequency-gaining tool. But the cost is low. Of course, there will be some time invested in setting these relationships up. On the other hand, it also gives you an opportunity to sell your products to the other merchants with whom you are cross-promoting. After all, they have to think about retirement as well. It forces you to network.

BOB: What about those fields in which the salesperson or professional can't come right out and publicly cross-promote? How might that situation be handled?

Regarding professionals, one example of a really soft cross-promotion is a doctor who provided hypertension screening as a free service on the premises at a grocery store. It was good for the store because it could advertise the fact that the doctor was going to do this free service. Meanwhile, the doctor obtained the actual test kits free from a pharmaceutical company. It was a great way for this doctor to build up his practice without offending his peers. So it was not blatant advertising, but more like a community involvement project. It was a very effective way of getting him in front of those potential customers, or patients.

BOB: What about professionals, such as a doctor and an accountant, cross-promoting with each other in a very low-key way?

JEFF: An easy way to do a soft cross-promotion is in your waiting room. Let's say you're an accountant, and you want to reach a doctor's patients, to sell your accounting services. If you do a newsletter, that could be put in the doctor's waiting room for patients to read. Simple little things such as that are very effective. Of course, the doctor's newsletter could be put in the accountant's waiting room as well. The same situation could be done with an attorney. You find ways of subtly infiltrating one another's customer base.

BOB: What about doctors suggesting that if their patients called their attorney or accountant and used their name, they could get a few minutes of advice without being charged?

JEFF: Throughout the relationship, let's say you are an attorney and you're networking with an accountant with whom you'd like to cross-promote. You offer an arrangement whereby somebody can call the accountant with a quick question for a limited time for a 30-day free trial. And the accountant's clients can call the attorney and ask a quick question. This way you get each other's clients to actually call. That is your initial lead for converting them to being your clients.

BOB: Let's take one more example and pretend we have a person selling a copy machine. The copy machine sales business is very competitive. We must get at least three or four of these salespeople a month in this office. How could they cross-promote in order to successfully get appointments with the decision makers?

JEFF: One really effective cross-promotion that comes to mind is actually more of an internal cross-promotion, which was done by a copy machine company in my hometown of Columbus, Ohio. At the same time, it crossed over to another area called community involvement. They ran a contest.

The idea was to get businesses to simply fill out a four-question survey. If they did, then $2 would be donated by the copy machine company to a certain charity. Whichever employee got the most questionnaires filled out would win some sort of prize. But all the lead money, the referral fees, as such, were being donated to charity. Here's what happened: A company repair person, not a salesperson, was fixing a copy machine upstairs from us. He went around to a bunch of offices, eventually getting to ours. He told us about the contest and said that if we would simply answer these four or five questions, then $2 would be donated to this charity.

While normally I would not talk to anybody, since this was for charity, I decided to answer the questions. The company had actually managed to get its repair people prospecting for the salespeople. Of course, the questions were basic, designed simply to see if they needed to follow up. Again, most people would answer the few questions because $2 was being donated to charity. So, as you can see, a cross-promotion with a nonprofit organization is a great idea because everybody wins.

The other thing is to develop relationships with those selling noncompetitive items to the same prospects—perhaps computer salespeople, telephone salespeople, and office furniture salespeople. I would develop a networking relationship with salespeople in my territory who were doing that, and what we would do is share.

Let's say I'm in an office on a cold call. The prospect is not interested in a copy machine because she has a brand new one, but in talking with her, I discover a need for a product or service she could buy from one of my networking buddies, and I ask if she'd like to hear from that person. And if it's a situation where I do make the sale, one or two more questions can determine if the prospect is also in need of one of the other products or services. If all of us are doing that for each other, we're getting a four-for-one prospecting deal.

Now, what about you. What can you, the reader, work out with somebody or some business that will be win-win? It isn't always easy to come up with a viable idea, and depending upon your business, it can't necessarily be in the form of a discount certificate. But brainstorm with those in your network, and come up with some ideas. You'll hit upon a winner sooner or later, and, as we learned from Jeff Slutsky, the payoff can be great.

Key Points

- "Streetfighting," according to author Jeff Slutsky, is a descriptive term used to illustrate an attitude toward marketing, promotion, and sales, based on outthinking, not outspending, the competition.

- A cross-promotion is basically a win-win promotion between salespeople or merchants who are trying to reach the same customers. There are different types of cross-promotions.

  1. *One-way cross-promotions.* You will provide certificates to your

cross-promotion partner, who will hand them out to his or her customers upon purchase.

2. *Two-way cross-promotions.* Essentially, "I'll hand out yours and you hand out mine."

3. *Reverse cross-promotions.* Your cross-promotion partner supplies you with the certificates, which you hand out to your customer upon purchase as an added value for buying from you.

- A huge advantage of the cross-promotion is this: not only does it cost nothing except for a little bit of quick printing but it is extremely targeted to the audience you want to reach.

- With just a bit of creativity, everyone from the direct salesperson to the professional can use cross-promotions to their advantage.

- One advantage of cross-promotions to the direct salesperson is that they are an excellent way to get face-to-face with an ordinarily difficult-to-reach decision maker.

- Cross-promotions are also an excellent closing tool.

- Professionals (doctors, lawyers, accountants, etc.) can often utilize soft cross-promotions as a way of sending prospects to one another.

- Internal cross-promotions get everyone else in the company (non-salespeople) prospecting for leads.

12

The Foundation
of Effective
Communication

I'd like to begin this chapter by sharing with you a recent incident. I believe it is the quintessential example of how easy it is to either get along, or not get along, with others. It shows just how much power each of us truly has to add positively or negatively to our network and to our world. Here's what happened.

My neighbor Carol, a staff supervisor for a local midsized business, called to invite me to a local dinner theater. As a holiday bonus her company had decided to send the entire staff to the theater for a night of fine food and entertainment, and Carol invited me to come as her guest.

Because the person with the tickets had not yet arrived, the manager would not let us into the main dining area to sit down and begin eating. Instead, he politely asked us to wait at the bar. Nursing a soft drink, I waited with the rest, when I sensed the first sign of trouble.

Carol announced she was not happy with the situation. She wanted us to begin eating right away so that we'd have plenty of time to enjoy our food. As far as Carol was concerned, the manager knew we were simply waiting for the person with the tickets to arrive, so "Why couldn't we just go in there now?" (I happened to have been in total agreement with Carol, but as a guest, I felt it wasn't my place to say so).

Then Carol said the magic words—the words that told me I was absolutely right to sense trouble. "I'm going to raise a fuss about this!" Oh no, I thought. This was supposed to be a fun, relaxing evening.

Carol summoned the manager over and began to verbally assault him. Well, he got stubborn and simply repeated, "Ma'am, it's against the rules. As far as I know, the person with the tickets may want to assign the seats." And every time Carol countered with an insult to his intelligence (or lack thereof), he countered with the same excuse.

I came to an executive decision: enough was enough. When Carol finally took a breath between words, I simply, and with a smile, politely asked the manager, "Sir, aside from the seating arrangements, would there be any other reason why seating us now would be uncomfortable for you?" He replied, "Not at all."

Praying to myself that Carol would not interrupt, which I could sense she was genuinely contemplating, I continued, "Well, I understand exactly how you feel, and in a similar situation I might feel the same way. Let me ask, if we were to assume total responsibility for the seating assignments—in fact, if I could get the staff supervisor herself to agree that you would be totally off the hook—would you consider letting us go in now?"

He responded with a smile and said, "That wouldn't be a problem." I replied, "Great, because being able to eat our meal without having to hurry would certainly add to our enjoyment of the show. And by the way, I appreciate your help and understanding." How did he respond? "My pleasure." As a matter of fact, at that point he personally escorted us to our seats and then checked on our comfort several times throughout the evening.

Carol was delighted and amazed. "How did you do that? What's your secret?"

"There is no secret," I answered. "It's simply a philosophy. An attitude and a decision to genuinely care about someone else's needs so that they, in turn, *want* to care about yours."

Incidents such as the above occur in my life quite often. I'm known as a person who can get people to do things for me that they ordinarily wouldn't do for others. The objective is a win-win outcome. As mentioned earlier in this book, isn't that really what networking is all about?

And my techniques for pulling off the seemingly impossible, ranging from extinguishing possible verbal and emotional fires to getting civil servants to cut through red tape and get things done for me quickly, is also a learned skill. Because I had the very best teacher! You see, there are probably only a few people in the history of the universe who have ever had *natural* people skills to the extent of a Dale Carnegie. One was Dale Carnegie himself; the other is my dad, Mike Burg.

He is one of the world's greatest natural networkers, one of those rare human beings who, despite his more-than-humble beginnings, has helped change the lives of many and positively affected the lives of many others. With everything I've learned and experienced regarding networking in the business sense, what I've learned about networking in the *human* sense has proven many times as valuable.

As we discuss certain philosophies and techniques in this chapter, I'll combine some of the thoughts and lessons I've learned from my dad, as well as from other "people experts," both modern and ancient.

Make People Feel Good About Themselves

Probably my dad's greatest strength is his ability to make those with whom he comes into contact feel important as human beings. And he does this not through manipulation or false compliments, but by genuine caring. We touched on that in Chapter 2 when we discussed asking feel-good questions that get people talking about themselves. But this philosophy goes much deeper than that. It's realizing that when we look at a person, what we and the rest of the world see is not necessarily the whole truth.

The business Dad founded and ran was a gymnasium school called the Academy of Physical and Social Development. This was a unique, psychodynamically oriented gymnasium school that helped countless individuals and families learn to communicate more effectively with each other. It was based on Dad's philosophy that if you could make a person feel good about himself, he would lead a healthy and productive life. Word got around about the success of the Academy and this resulted in a *Time* magazine feature story.

While I was growing up, I watched all sorts of people come into the Academy. I'd see a family walk in: the man, big and handsome; the woman, pretty and trim, with an air of confidence; the child, attractive and well-dressed, looking like a million bucks. They looked like the all-American family.

But when you got to know them, you realized that this guy with muscles didn't *feel* so strong, this pretty woman didn't *feel* attractive, and the youngster was not happy being their child. You realized that there was more to this than met the eye, and that only when people feel good about themselves do they feel strong and pretty. And when they are successful and make their parents happy with them, they feel very welcome in the family.

The Academy had a motto that I feel is timeless: "To have a body does not make one a man. To have a child does not make one a parent." What we see is not always what we get, and we need to approach people as individuals whose lives we can somehow make better by making them feel better about themselves.

This philosophy is easy to relate to networking, isn't it? After all, what comes to mind when we approach center-of-influence types? They might *appear* to have it all together. We know they might be successful in business, have lots of friends around them, and appear to be always happy. Yet, below the surface, things may not be so wonderful.

Think about it. We don't know what is going on with their family. We don't know what their pressures of business are at that time. We don't really know what's in their heads, and as a result, they can use a lot of good, positive strokes. And, if done in a sincere, genuine manner, they are going to be very grateful because it's going to make them feel good. That is where confidence comes in. The more confident this person feels, the more he is going to appreciate your coming into his life.

Five Questions of Life

Dad's mentor, so to speak, was a post-Biblical sage by the name of ben Zoma, whose philosophy dealt with different states of being and appreciation, as expressed through four basic questions. Dad later added a fifth question, which followed along the same lines.

Question 1: Who Is a Wise Person?

ben Zoma's answer to this first question was, "One who learns from others."

How many famous quotes and sayings run along those same lines? For example, "We have two ears and only one mouth for a reason." Isn't that true? When we talk, we must be saying something that we already know (or think we know). Only by listening can we become wiser in whatever situation we happen to be involved.

Let's take, for example, a doctor. A patient comes into his or her office looking sick. Regardless of the numerous years of education and vast amount of knowledge this doctor has concerning medicine and the human body, the easiest way to get to the root of the patient's problem is for the doctor to first ask about and *listen* to what the patient describes as symptoms. Only then can the doctor intelligently suggest a particular treatment.

In networking we can relate this question to that person who actively listens to other people. What do they feel? How do they feel? Why do they feel? What's working in their life or business, and what isn't? As we find their needs, we know what direction to take with them. If a doctor provides a diagnosis and prescription without first knowing the symptoms, that's malpractice. If we, as salespeople, try and sell a product or service to someone without first knowing his true needs, isn't that malpractice as well?

Question 2: Who Is a Mighty Person?

"One who can control his or her emotions and make of an enemy a friend," says ben Zoma.

This means nothing more than having enough self-control and discipline to take a bad situation and make it work for you. Imagine approaching someone who isn't particularly friendly or open, but having enough strength or be mighty enough to turn that person to your side. And usually, when we can win people over and turn them in our direction, they turn out to be our biggest supporters.

Abraham Lincoln once said, "I don't like that person—I'm going to have to get to know him better." How many friendships do you currently have with others that began in sort of less-than-amiable fashion? If you have one, several, or many, you know that those are some of your most rewarding relationships. If you have none, then set a goal to try to turn one "enemy" into a friend. Just one at first. Watch what happens. I assure you, the results will be habit-forming.

Question 3: Who Is a Rich Person?

A truly rich person is one who appreciates his or her lot. In other words, somebody who is happy with himself, somebody who really feels good enough about his life and lifestyle that he can be a pretty complete or contented person.

Of course, the standard response to that question from most people is "Someone who has money." And certainly there's nothing wrong with having money. It's just that money, in and of itself, can only make a person wealthy. It can't make one rich.

In relation to networking, this would translate into a person who appreciates and enjoys the individuals in his or her network, even if not yet receiving immediate referrals from those people.

Question 4: Who Is an Honored Person?

One who honors others, one who makes others feel good about themselves, is herself an honored person. In networking, this means liking and caring about your networking prospects enough so that they feel it. In turn, they will honor you. Here's a good practice exercise: next time you are at a social or business function, begin introducing people to each other. Have a one-sentence, complimentary statement about everyone you introduce. As you *honor* everyone you introduce (even by just taking the time to make the introduction) watch how you become the hit of the function. It works every time.

Question 5: Who Is a Brave Person?

This question is my father's. A brave person is one who is smart enough to be afraid and still do their job. According to Dad, "I've met a lot of people, both during the war and outside of the service, who were willing to physically fight it out. Although they were willing to go into battle, so to speak, to do things others might not do, they really did not have the sense of appreciation of themselves. They weren't scared because they didn't have a reason to be scared. They didn't know enough to be scared. They didn't have anything to be scared about.

"While you have to give those people credit for what they do, it's the person who has real feelings about being scared and goes ahead anyway, trying to accomplish what he or she set out to do, who deserves a real pat on the back."

How does that relate to networking? Simply this: it is the true networker who, though smart enough to recognize potential rejection, still reaches out to give of himself or herself.

Truth, Justice, Peace, and Love

Four ingredients that add to a successful networking recipe are truth, justice, peace, and love. Although my feelings about these four can be argued semantically, you'll see where the philosophies fit into the style of the successful networker throughout this book.

Truth: What is vital to realize is that truth (or the correct way of doing things) in your own mind doesn't necessarily mean that the person you're dealing with sees the truth in the same way. And, unless you are transacting with someone who can communicate in a positive way, a lack of communication or negative communication will be the result: hostile feelings or misunderstandings that will not work for the benefit of any of the parties concerned.

My friend and fellow speaker Jim Cathcart, author of *Relationship Selling*, explains what he calls the Platinum Rule. The Golden Rule, of course, is "Do unto others as you would have them do unto you." According to Jim, the Platinum Rule is "Do unto others as *they* want to be done unto."

In other words, just because we, in our mind, see the perfect business relationship being a certain way and following certain rules or procedures, that doesn't mean the other person feels the same way. What is the truth? As far as I'm concerned, if we want a positive business relationship with that person, we must try to see the truth from *that person's* point of view.

Justice: This is maturity. It's the ability to say, "Hey, I'm wrong. I can do something about it, and I *will* do something about it. I will change." In networking we must be able to admit when we are wrong. So many confrontations occur and continue because of the inability to admit shortcomings, when admitting those shortcomings will only make you more of a hero in the other person's eyes.

Peace: Peace comes about when there is comfort and a lack of stress when dealing with people. You're not afraid to say things to them; you're not under pressure, because if there is any kind of misunderstanding about the truth, you will be able to work it out. People are willing to deal with the justice that accompanies understanding. In networking, peace results from two or more people having a mutual respect.

Love: This means putting the other person ahead of yourself. The other person becomes more important to you than yourself. In networking, realistically, we don't love our networking prospects as we love our own families, but we care about them, their families, and their needs, which in return will influence them to have good feelings about us.

From what I've experienced, putting another person's needs ahead of one's own seems to be a struggle few are able to overcome. Too many people ask themselves, "How does doing that benefit me?" I can only say that the successful networkers I know, the ones receiving tons of referrals and feeling truly happy about themselves, continually put the other person's needs ahead of their own. Let me say this one more time because it is so important:

> The successful networkers I know, the ones receiving tons of referrals and feeling truly happy about themselves, continually put the other person's needs ahead of their own.

Do You Network as a Parent, Adult, or Child?

In the best-selling book *Games People Play,* author Eric Berne, often credited with being the father of transactional analysis, points out three distinct personality states: Parent, Adult, and Child. These are states taken on and displayed by each of us, depending upon what we are feeling at that particular point in time. The following is my paraphrased explanation of these three states and how they relate to networking.

The Child in all of us is the victim. He or she feels like a baby, put down, blamed, punished, controlled. As a result, the person is angry and looking to get even. And usually the Child wants to get even with the person who assumes the Parent role.

The Parent in all of us is usually a victim of our own upbringing, biases, and environment. People in the Parent role mean well; they just don't recognize negative communication. They don't realize that they're putting somebody down. They don't realize that they're making somebody feel bad.

The Adult in all of us, which is the ideal, is the negotiator, the communicator—the respectful, honest, active listener who's trustworthy and just. And somebody you would just love doing business with.

Isn't it a fact that we have all three of those situations in the networking process? There are people who talk down to us. They are the Parent and we are the Child. In that situation we have to know that it's not something to be taken personally, but that we have to bring ourselves up to the Adult level. At the same time, we have to make sure we don't come across like the Parent talking down to them as the Child, but as Adult to Adult.

It's also important to keep in mind that you can't expect prospects to act like adults just because *you* know how to. So don't feel put down if they can't respond that way. I realize that is easier said than done. The way to overcome that is to make a game out of it. Be aware the next time you are in a negative transaction, and see if you can *win*. Of course, you don't win by emotionally *beating* that person, but by *building* that person to an Adult level, in order to match the level to which you have risen.

Networking Disciplines

Networking discipline says that if you don't abide by networking techniques, you won't get all the referrals you are capable of getting. If you do, you will get referrals—lots and lots of them. Let's number the seven networking disciplines right down the line:

First, get the necessary knowledge needed to effectively network. Review the techniques you've learned throughout this book until you really know them, because the more you practice, the better you are going to feel and the more effective you're going to be. The same goes for other books you read and tapes you listen to.

Second, place yourself in front of potential networking prospects. Understand that you can have fear and anxiety and still be brave enough to do it and be effective. We all have trepidations when going into a room full of people we don't know. And we've all experienced rejection and don't enjoy the feeling. Despite this, we can succeed. Realize that the more you practice, the easier it is to face any new situation. Also know that the more new situations you face, the less intimidating they become.

Third, be wise by learning from others, especially your networking prospects, and learn how you can help *them.*

Fourth, give unrequited referrals. Help the others in your network without expecting an immediate payback. Don't look for a "shake" just because you're being effective and good about your actions.

Fifth is tact. This is so important! Tact is the language of strength. If we could listen on tape to what we say in everyday conversations, we'd be amazed at the lack of tact and sensitivity in the way we relate to others. There's a great deal of truth in the old saying, "You can catch more flies with honey than you can with vinegar." Make an agreement with yourself to analyze the way you talk to others for just 21 days. Watch your improvement every day and be proud of yourself.

Sixth, allow yourself to be rewarded with endless referrals after showing persistence. Follow through in gratitude.

And seventh, realize that discipline and networking are nothing more than learning how to benefit from being the "boss of yourself" so you may constructively help and influence others to network. Only *you* can determine how you are going to handle an individual person or situation. By being the boss of yourself, you control the situation, and your own success, while adding positively to those whose lives you touch. As my dad says, "We are ideally put on earth to help others." And as we help others, we eventually and invariably help ourselves.

As a postscript to this chapter, let me point out that, regardless of what you are used to doing, regardless of the way you presently handle conflict with others, effective communication is a *learned skill.* Fellow speaker and author Anthony Robbins says, "Your past does not equal your future." No matter what your shortcomings in communicating and networking with others have been, you can use the techniques presented in this book to begin developing a powerful network of contacts.

Even the story I began with about my neighbor, Carol, who was looking for a fight with the theater manager, contains a lesson. How can you use that as a guide for turning potential lemons into lemonade—or potential enemies into friends?

Living your life from a perspective of strength is a lot more fun and rewarding. Do we need to continually work at this in order to make it effective? Yes! And it's worth it.

Key Points

- Whenever possible, make others feel good about themselves.

- People are not always what they seem to be.

- To have a body does not make one a man. To have a child does not make one a parent.

- These are the five questions of life:
  1. *Who is a wise person?* One who learns from others.
  2. *Who is a mighty person?* One who can control his or her emotions and make of an enemy a friend.
  3. *Who is a rich person?* One who appreciates his or her lot.
  4. *Who is an honored person?* One who honors others.
  5. *Who is a brave person?* One who is smart enough to be afraid and still do their job.

- The four key ingredients in a successful networking recipe are truth, justice, peace, and love.

- The successful networkers I know, the ones receiving tons of referrals and feeling truly happy about themselves, continually put the other person's needs ahead of their own.

- We each display three personality states:
  1. *The Child:* The Child feels like the victim, like a baby—put down, blamed, punished, controlled.
  2. *The Parent:* The Parent means well but is domineering and controlling.
  3. *The Adult:* The Adult is the ideal—the negotiator, the communicator, win-win–oriented.

- There are seven networking disciplines:
  1. Acquire knowledge.
  2. Place yourself in front of potential networking prospects.

3. Be wise by learning from others—especially your networking prospects. Learn how you can help them.
4. Give unrequited referrals. Help others in your network without expecting an immediate payback.
5. Be tactful. Tact is the language of strength.
6. Allow yourself to be rewarded with endless referrals after showing persistence. Follow through in gratitude.
7. Realize that discipline and networking are nothing more than learning how to benefit from being the "boss of yourself" so that you can constructively help and influence others to network. We are ideally put on earth to help others. And, of course, as we help others we invariably help ourselves.

13

Remember Names and Faces for Profit

We are all so vain that we love to have our names remembered by those who have met us but once. We exaggerate the talents and virtues of those who can do this, and we are ready to repay their powers with lifelong devotion. The ability to associate in the mind names and faces is a tremendous asset to a politician, and it will prolong the pastorate of any clergyman.

WILLIAM LYONS PHELPS

I would like to add one thought to Mr. Phelps's splendid observation. Not only will we repay those powers with lifelong devotion, but with our business dollars and referrals as well.

Really, don't you feel good when someone remembers your name when you least expect it? For instance, when I visited a car dealership for the second time 3 weeks later, the salesperson called me by name. At that point, he increased his chances of making the sale. Why? Because he made me feel important, as though my business mattered. As if my coming back was reason to stand up and take notice. We all like to feel important, don't we?

The legendary Dale Carnegie agrees: "Remember that a person's name is to him or her the sweetest and most important sound in any language." Whether it should be that way or not doesn't matter, because that is simply the way it is. The people who best capitalize on this aspect of human vanity have the greatest chances of "winning friends and influencing people" (in Mr. Carnegie's own words) and in turn dramatically increasing their referral business.

During my seminars, I often relate the story of the time I was dragged off to a local party. I am not a party person. I speak for a living. The last thing in the world I want to do for relaxation is speak.

On those rare occasions when, for one reason or another, I can't refuse the invitation, I will somehow find a way to amuse myself. Usually by enjoying the hors d'oeuvres and remembering the names of everyone I meet...to myself!

At this one particular party, a person who had attended one of my seminars blabbed to the group that I could probably go through the entire room telling everyone's name. I do that during many of my seminars. It wasn't, however, something I normally do at social gatherings.

Fortunately, I had been locking in the names; otherwise, I could have been very embarrassed. I called back everybody's name, and for the rest of the evening, yours truly was the hit of the party. I'm not the type who usually is. People were surrounding me, asking how I did it. They gave me their cards and wanted mine. I'm relating this story not to brag but to make a point.

I don't do my networking locally anymore, but if I did, I would have had a whole bunch of serious prospects from that party. They were fascinated. Certainly not by me, but by the fact that I could remember all of their names. And there were over 50 people there! Talk about turning a social function into networking!

And again, the success lies in remembering people's names and faces. I know a lot of us will say "I'm really good when it comes to remembering faces, but not names." Well, that's fine, but it isn't enough. Let's face it, using the techniques from the other chapters, you've worked hard to establish the relationship.

When you see this person again, away from the context in which you met, and say, " You know I remember your face, but I can't remember your name," it just isn't the same. Certainly not nearly as impressive as calling that person by name. Many of us with naturally poor memories have learned to compensate by practicing the techniques I will describe in this chapter.

You Can Do It, Too

So many people are totally convinced, as I was at one time, that mastering the skill, or even improving it, is next to impossible. Well, it isn't. In fact, it's not only possible, but fun as well.

Let us first take a quick moment to answer one of my most often asked questions: "Why is it I can remember faces but not names?" Good question! Here's the answer. The reason faces are memorable is because they are tangible. You certainly wouldn't look at a person and say, "You know, I remember your name, but I can't quite remember your face," would you? Of course not. And why? Because, again, faces are tangible; faces have handles.

Names, on the other hand, are intangible. They cannot be seen. They are merely sounds. When we walk up to a person we have met previously, we still see the same face, but not the name. What we need to learn how to do is not only see that person's name (and I'm not talking about name tags), but be able to connect it with that person's face as well.

Just Follow These Steps

In order to make name-face connections effectively, we must follow these six steps (please glance at them quickly, and then continue):

1. Observe the person's outstanding facial feature.
2. Exaggerate the person's outstanding facial feature.
3. Observe the person's name.
4. Repeat the person's name (in order to ensure you heard it correctly).
5. Form a mental picture of what the name suggests, or a "sound-alike" (a similar sound or word that takes something you cannot picture and turns it into something you *can* picture).
6. Form a ridiculous association between the mental picture suggested by the name (or sound-alike) and the outstanding facial feature.

Let's take each of these steps individually and see how they lead to the mastery of this very important networking skill.

Observe the Person's Outstanding Facial Feature

When I use the term "outstanding facial feature," I do not necessarily mean the outstandingly *good* feature or outstandingly *bad* feature— simply the feature on that person's face that stands out the most or is most prominent.

An outstanding facial feature could be almost anything: big eyes, small eyes, deep-set eyes, almond-shaped eyes, big nose, small nose, pug nose, thin eyebrows, thick eyebrows, wrinkly forehead, high forehead, thin face, long face, round face, small scar, big scar, thin lips, thick lips, character lines from the nose, dimple, mustache, beard, bald head, curly hair, square chin, high cheekbones, low cheekbones, freckles—the list goes on and on.

In fact, the list is almost limitless, depending on how diligently you look. Just a friendly warning, however: at first the task may seem difficult. We may even ask ourselves, "Hey, what am I going to do? This person doesn't have an outstanding facial feature. His face is totally plain." Well, don't worry. That person does, in fact, have an outstanding facial feature. It is simply a matter of getting used to finding it, which gets easier and easier with practice.

Exaggerate the Person's Outstanding Facial Feature

Now that we have isolated the person's outstanding facial feature, we need to exaggerate it and use our imagination to really make it stand out. In other words, if the person has big eyes, see those eyes as being huge. If he has a thin face, see that face as being so thin that a toothpick would have trouble hiding behind it. If she has a scar, then see that scar as being extremely deep. Whatever the person's outstanding facial feature, simply see it as being much more than it really is.

Observe the Person's Name

An important, if not obvious, step is to observe the person's name. I know, that sounds simple, but how many times do we overlook doing that for one reason or another? Maybe we're not concentrating. Possibly we are so used to forgetting names that we've stopped trying to pay attention. Then there is the seeming difficulty of being able to picture that person's name, a skill we will master very soon. From now on, please observe the person's name when you hear it.

Repeat the Person's Name

The main reason for repeating the name is to ensure you heard it correctly the first time. For instance, if you didn't quite get the name, the person will feel complimented that you cared enough to ask, and that you remembered it correctly the next time.

You can also repeat the name once or twice during the conversation just to get familiar and comfortable with it. "Nice to meet you, Mr. and Mrs. Kozlowski." Simply repeat the name once when you hear it, and then maybe once or twice during the actual conversation, and once again when ending the conversation.

Form a Mental Picture of What
the Name Suggests

Remember, a sound-alike is a similar sound or word that will take something you cannot picture and turn it into something you can picture. The sound-alike will simply serve as a reminder of the real name.

There are many names that easily present pictures. Take a look at the names in the left column of Table 13.1. Each of these names suggests pictures that we can easily see. On the other hand, there are many, many names that by themselves do not present pictures. A short list of these appears in the right column of Table 13.1. A longer list (1000 of them to be exact) appears at the end of this chapter. These sound-alikes are simply my suggestions. You may use them or come up with your own.

They are yours to familiarize yourself with and to make mastering this name-remembering system much faster and easier. You will find that you do not have to rely on hard-core rote memory.

As long as you are familiar and comfortable with how the difficult-to-picture names become items you can picture, the purpose will be served. I have also included 100 first names as well as various "standards" for different parts of names. The same will hold true with these as with the last names.

Join the Name With the Face

The sixth and final step is what really ties it all together. Form a ridiculous association between the mental picture suggested by the name, or sound-alike, and the outstanding facial feature. For practice, let's meet some people right now. We don't even need to actually look at their faces at this time; you will picture them easily. I'll walk you through the first two, then ask you to try some on your own.

Let's pretend that you are about to be introduced to a woman who has somewhat deep-set eyes. Before you are even introduced to her, you observe that her outstanding facial feature happens to be those deep-set eyes. Now exaggerate the outstanding facial feature, and see this woman's eyes being *extremely* deep set. Her eyes become so deep set they are way back in their sockets.

As the two of you shake hands, you note her telling you that her name is Joan Forrest. Don't concern yourself with her first name for the moment. Now repeat her name so it fits naturally into the conversation, such as, "It's very nice to meet you, Ms. Forrest."

The next step is to form a mental picture of what the name suggests, or, if the name doesn't suggest anything you can easily picture, decide upon a sound-alike that will work. In this case, the name Forrest is

Table 13.1. Picturing a Name

Names that suggest pictures	Names that need sound-alikes
Taylor	Gordon: Garden
Horne	Kakish: Cactus
Carr	Sullivan: Sell a van
Frost	Foster: Force tear
Sanders	Colletti: Call a tea
Walker	Garrett: Carrot
Coleman	Marcott: My cot
Miller	Nixon: Nicks on, mixin'
Hunter	Henderson: Hand her some
Forrest	Quigley: Wiggly
Rose	Martin: My tin
Hill	Harackiewicz: Hairy carrots
Pierce	James: Games
Colby	Thibodeau: Tip a doe
·Wolfe	Van Vliet: Van fleet
Silverman	Zarkin: Far in, parkin'
Carpenter	Connolly: Corn'l leave
	Bennett: Pen net
	Frazier: Razor
	Simon: Dime in
	Rondeau: Run doe
	Berrisano: Berry sand o
	Murphy: More peas
	Kaplan: Cap land
	Leonhardt: Lean hard
	Jones: Stones
	Giagregorio: gin in cracked cargo
	Malinowski: Mail on a ski
	Sannicandro: Sunny can grow

easy to picture, isn't it? Simply picture a forest. The fact that the two words are not spelled exactly alike does not even come into play. Picturing a forest will work just fine.

Now, form a ridiculous association between the forest and her deep-set eyes. I would see those deep-set eyes of Ms. Forrest actually being a huge forest with thousands and thousands of gigantic trees in them. I would also try to put myself into that picture by walking around in there and possibly getting lost.

A fairly easy one, isn't it? However, be especially careful with the easy pictures. Surprisingly, the easy pictures are the ones we forget, because we tend to not concentrate as hard on them.

Let's try another one. This time, the person you are about to meet is a man whose outstanding feature happens to be character lines coming from each side of his nose. In reality they are not especially deep. Since they are his outstanding facial feature, however, you see them in your mind's eye as being extremely deep.

You observe him tell you that his name is Dave Frazier. You respond by repeating his name, and then you immediately decide if Frazier is a name you can picture, or one that needs a sound-alike. In this case, a sound-alike appears to be needed, doesn't it? It would be awfully difficult to picture a "frazier."

You might be thinking, "What about Joe Frazier, the former heavy-weight boxing champion. Or even my good friend who also happens to be named Frazier?" Although there are different theories regarding the use of celebrities or friends with the same name as the person we are trying to remember, I personally discourage it.

Why? Because it can get confusing. If someone you meet for the first time is named Steven Lewis, and you picture Jerry Lewis, that might be fine while he is still right in front of you. But chances are that when you see that person again the next day or week, you won't be sure whether he told you his name was Mr. Lewis or Mr. Martin (as in Dean). You might remember that you pictured a celebrity, but which one?

Back to Mr. Frazier. A good sound-alike for Frazier is "razor." It sounds enough like the real name to serve as a reminder yet is much easier to picture. Now you must make a weird association between the character lines and the razor. If I were making the association, I might see Mr. Frazier as having no character lines until I shaved him with my gigantic razor. And of course the more I shaved, the deeper those character lines became.

Or you might see yourself trying as hard as you can to shave off his character lines with your gigantic razor. Whichever association you use, you need to really see the picture clearly in your mind's eye. Even see the details of the particular razor—color, brand, size, and so on. Be aware that the association you yourself make is the one that will work best.

Let's Continue, Even Without Any Pictures

Now I will give you the outstanding facial features and then the names of eight people. Make sure to go through all six steps with each person (yes, even repeating the name out loud). After this exercise, we will review all 10 to see how you did.

I will give you the associations I would have made for these eight. If, however, you think you have one that would work better, then please use it. If these seem difficult at all, please don't worry! You are learning something new. I am concerned not with the number you get right, but that you begin to feel more comfortable with the process.

The next person you are about to meet is a woman with hairy eyebrows. Her name is Hazel Gold. Have you done the first five steps? All right, let's make the association. See her hairy eyebrows filled with thousands of gigantic nuggets of gold. Can't you see yourself just taking all those nuggets of gold right out of Ms. Gold's hairy eyebrows? You should be very wealthy after doing that!

You are about to meet a gentleman with a very round face. His name is Tim Simon. A good sound-alike for Simon is "dime in." See Mr. Simon's face being so round because it was stuffed (possibly by you, to make the association even more meaningful) with lots and lots of gigantic dimes. You are the one who kept stuffing dimes in his face. Now imagine his round face getting skinnier and skinnier as the dimes begin shooting out of his face.

The next person is a woman with dimples on both sides of her face. Her name is Mary Garrett. For Garrett, you might want to picture a "carrot." Garrett and carrot sound alike, don't they? In your mind's eye, you can picture a gigantic carrot sticking out of each of her dimples. The already huge carrots continue to grow larger and larger. Really force yourself to see this picture. It gets easier with practice.

Now you are about to meet a man with a very scraggly mustache. This brings up the question, "How can facial hair count when it might not be there the next time you see him?" I will answer that question with another question. How about the situation where a man shaves off his mustache or beard and it's about a week before you realized he's shaved? Has that ever happened to you? Amazing but true, isn't it? Because of that phenomenon, facial hair does count as an outstanding facial feature.

So this man's outstanding facial feature is his scraggly mustache. His name is Mark Taylor. Simply picture a very skillful tailor mending Mr. Taylor's scraggly mustache. Make sure you can see the picture, and make it as silly and illogical as you possibly can.

Our next person is a woman whose outstanding facial feature is her high cheekbones. Her name is Eileen Rose. See yourself planting hundreds of roses in her high cheekbones. After finally getting them all planted, one by one they begin to fall out. Of course, you do your best to replant them. Silly? Definitely! The sillier the better.

Let's introduce ourselves to a gentleman who has an extremely pointy nose. His name is Norman Kakish. We need a sound-alike for Kakish, don't we? Picturing "cactus" will do just fine. Let's use substitution to remember his name and imagine that pointy nose actually being a cactus. If you touch it, you will probably prick your finger on one of the needles. The sound-alike cactus should remind you of his real name, which is Kakish.

Your business associate is about to introduce you to a gentleman whose outstanding facial feature is his receding hairline. His name is Paul Walker. Make that association by seeing yourself walking on the top of his forehead. You did this for so long that he lost all of the hair he had in that area. Now he has a receding hairline. Really picture it.

Finally, you are about to meet a woman with very tiny ears. She tells you her name is Terri Malinowski. A sound-alike for Malinowski might be "mail on a ski." Try to imagine the difficulty a piece of mail would have skiing down Ms. Malinowski's tiny ears. Try to make that ridiculous picture really come alive. You might have even used "melon ow ski" for your sound-alike and pictured a melon yelling "Ow!" as it attempted to ski down Ms. Malinowski's tiny ears.

I Bet You Remember Them

All right, we have met a total of 10 people, without the benefit of even seeing their faces. Here is what I would like you to do. Go back to the first introduction and very briefly review each of the associations, just concentrating on remembering the last names. Don't put too much pressure on yourself.

After your review, please fill in the blanks next to the outstanding facial features listed below. As you come to each outstanding facial feature, simply picture your association. Your true memory should then supply you with the correct name.

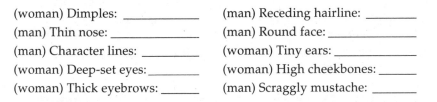

(woman) Dimples: _____   (man) Receding hairline: _____

(man) Thin nose: _____   (man) Round face: _____

(man) Character lines: _____   (woman) Tiny ears: _____

(woman) Deep-set eyes: _____   (woman) High cheekbones: _____

(woman) Thick eyebrows: _____   (man) Scraggly mustache: _____

How did you do? Did you get them all correct? Most of them? A few of them? None of them? Again, it doesn't matter. I just want you to get the hang of it. At the conclusion of the chapter, I will supply you with some good practice exercises that will help you to steadily improve your real-life names-and-faces abilities.

Just Like Learning to Drive a Car

Are you asking yourself, "Well, that's all fine and well. How, though, will I ever go through all six steps and still be able to carry on a halfway intelligent conversation with that person?" At this point, I am reminded of what I call the "standard shift" theory of remembering names and faces.

If you can drive a standard shift car, you will be able to relate to this analogy. Do you recall the very first time you attempted to drive a standard shift car? Crunch...lurch...stall. Wasn't that first hour something awful? If you were anything like me, you were so concerned with trying to coordinate the releasing of the clutch with the handling of the gear shift, you weren't actually going anywhere.

After that first hour, however, it was a bit easier, wasn't it? And it became progressively easier with each trip behind the wheel. Eventually, you were able to drive that car by instinct, the individual steps blending together as one fluid motion. This method of remembering names and faces works the same way.

First Names Are Even Easier

Now to learn how to remember people's first names. There are actually two ways, depending upon the circumstances. First, if you only need to remember the first name of the person you are meeting, simply use the exact same method you just learned for remembering the last name.

Only it will now be much easier, because compared to the number of last names you will eventually come across and have to turn into pictures, there are relatively few first names. At the end of the book, I've given you a list of 100 first names, half male, half female, and a suggested mental picture or sound-alike for each one.

There are other first names that are not on the list, but it does cover most of them. Run down the list several times just to familiarize yourself with these names. You will soon find it a snap to quickly associate any of them with a person's outstanding facial feature.

Let's return to the business world or any other situation where it would be more proper and certainly more impressive to remember both the first and last name. I have found, by the way, that most people (even if they won't admit it) appreciate being referred to by their last name, preceded, of course, by Mr. or Ms. Depending upon the situation, I personally address people by Mr. or Ms. until they ask me to

call them by their first name. I have been complimented for that practice. Besides, if I am going to err, I would rather do it on the side of
respect and courtesy. Here is how this is accomplished. Lock in the
person's last name exactly as you learned. Take the picture you now
have of the person's last name and associate that with the picture of
the first name. Let's do that for the 10 people we just met.

Joan Forrest.   For Joan, I use "groan." Your original picture is of
being lost in that forest. I don't know about you, but being lost in a
forest would certainly make me *groan* real loud.

Dave Frazier.   For Dave, I use "save." Go back to the picture of
shaving off those character lines with a razor (Frazier). Just keep
doing that; Mr. Frazier hopes someone will come along and *save* him
from any more.

Hazel Gold.   For Hazel, I simply picture a "hazelnut." We saw ourselves picking gigantic gold nuggets out of Ms. Gold's hairy eyebrows. Imagine that one of those nuggets turns out to be a *hazelnut*.
How disappointing, right?

Tim Simon.   For Tim, "tin" will work fine. We had seen the gigantic
dime in Mr. Simon's very round face. In fact, there were lots of
them, weren't there? Well, the strange thing about these dimes is
that they were all wrapped in *tin* foil.

Mary Garrett.   For Mary, I use "marry." Picture a ring or a wedding
veil. We know that gigantic carrots sticking out of Ms. Garrett's
dimples reminded us of her last name. In this instance I might say to
myself, "I sure wouldn't want to *marry* a woman who has gigantic
carrots sticking out of each of her dimples."

Mark Taylor.   For Mark, I use either "Magic Marker" or simply the
picture of a physical mark. In this instance, where it took a skillful
tailor to mend Mr. Taylor's scraggly mustache, I might just see him
taking his Magic Marker and marking up the spots that needed the
most repair.

Eileen Rose.   For Eileen, I just see myself leaning ("I lean"). You
might say to yourself, as you see this picture, "If *I lean* on all of those
roses, surely they will be crushed beyond repair."

Norman Kakish.   For Norman, I use "normal" and associate that
with the last name. For instance, in this particular case I might ask
myself, "If a nose like Mr. Kakish's was actually made out of *cactus*,
would that be *normal?*"

Paul Walker.   For Paul, I use "ball." You saw yourself walking on
the top of Mr. Walker's forehead. In fact, you did that for so long

that he lost all of the hair he had in that area. The result is a receding hairline, correct? Now you could also picture that while you were walking, you were bouncing a gigantic basket*ball*. I'm sure that didn't help his hair any.

Terri Malinowski. For Terri, I picture "terry cloth." Remember that mail on a ski? Or even the melon saying "Ow!" as it attempted to ski down those tiny ears? Whichever association you used, just put a *terry cloth* into the picture. And be sure to make it illogical.

Now let's quiz ourselves on the first names. I will give you the last names, and you fill in the blanks.

Garrett: _____   Kakish: _____

Forrest: _____   Simon: _____

Malinowski: _____   Frazier: _____

Walker: _____   Rose: _____

Taylor: _____   Gold: _____

If you really concentrated on either the associations I gave you or on your own, and if you allowed your imagination to run a bit wild, then I'm sure you scored high. If you're not quite satisfied with the results, review the associations one more time, then test yourself again. I know you will do even better.

Let's Meet Some *Real* Folks

If you did well in associating these people's last names with their out-standing facial features, then this next part will be even easier. Let's face it, you still had to imagine a face, and that isn't always easy. Now let's meet some people whose faces we can at least see, even if they are only two-dimensional pictures. Take a look at Figure 13.1. Real faces are actually much easier, once you become comfortable with this method.

With each person, you will have the first and last names, and sug-gested sound-alikes for last names (sound-alikes for first names are in the back of the book). Go through the six steps in order to remember each person's last name. Please make it a point to cover up the per-son's name until you observe and then exaggerate the outstanding facial feature. When you feel you know the person's last name, then lock in the first name.

After you do each of these yourself, look at the way I made the asso-ciations. Remember, if I seem to have the hang of it more than you

Tanya Reagan

Dianne Collibus

Don Carson

Ed Marconi

Gwendolyn Smith

Joanne Di Atillio

Bill McCue

James Conant

Figure 13-1. Real faces make it easy to imagine facial features.

right now, it's only because I have been doing it longer. You'll catch on. Don't worry. Besides, the following names are not exactly the easiest you will ever come across. I am attempting to make this as realistic a situation for you as possible.

Bill McCue.   The outstanding facial feature I used for Mr. McCue was his wide nose. I took *my cue* (McCue) stick and shoved it as hard as I could up his wide nose, which must have hurt! I'm sure he wanted to take a *pill* (Bill) in order to relieve the pain. Weird associations, but effective nonetheless. If your associations didn't work, then just go over them again, but make then even stronger this time. Or you can use mine.

Gwendolyn Smith.   I used the mark on the right side of her face as her outstanding facial feature. My standard for Smith is a blacksmith's hammer. For Gwendolyn, I use "dwindlin'." So the mark on Gwendolyn Smith's face was once very large, but now it's being chiseled out by the black*smith*'s hammer and is *dwindlin'* down in size.

Don Carson.   I immediately see the beard as being Mr. Carson's outstanding facial feature. The name Carson, if you divide it into syllables, presents the words (and picture) "car" and "sun." No sound-alike is needed. Let's put one of those old Matchbox cars in that beard, and see it being totally protected from the sun. My standard for the first name Don is "pawn," as you might find in a chess set. See that *car*, which is protected from the *sun*, being driven by a gigantic chess *pawn.*

Tanya Reagan.   You may have noticed Ms. Reagan's low cheekbones. Of course, you may not have. As you know, 10 or more of us could look at the same face and each see a different outstanding feature. But I used her low cheekbones, and for the name Reagan I used the sound-alike "ray gun." Ms. Reagan's cheekbones are sagging so low because you shot them with a *ray gun.* And the effect of the ray gun turned her cheekbones *tan* (Tanya).

James Conant.   The outstanding facial feature I see for Mr. Conant is his triangle-shaped face. In fact, what if you took a gigantic triangular ice cream cone, topped with ants instead of sprinkles, and voilà! you have your association. The standard I use for James is "games." See those *ants* on top of that *cone* playing lots of *games* in the ice cream.

Joanne Di Atillio.   I see Joanne's outstanding facial feature being her short, curly hair. For Di Atillio, I picture a gigantic golf *tee* (Di) *till*ing, or hoeing, a bunch of *O*'s. Really use your imagination for this one! For the first name, Joanne, I use "chowin'." In your mind's eye, picture Joanne *chowin'* on those *O*'s.

Ed Marconi. The shape of Mr. Marconi's face was what I saw as his outstanding facial feature. To me, his face sort of angles down into a square chin. The sound-alike for Marconi is "macaroni," so picture yourself pulling a gigantic piece of macaroni out of his face through that square chin. His first name is Ed, for which I use "egg." Just see that particular bit of pasta being *egg macaroni.*

Dianne Collibus. Ms. Collibus's outstanding facial feature is her small mouth. You need to find a bus to get to work, and you know there is one inside Ms. Collibus's mouth. Just *call a bus,* and one will probably drive right out of Ms. Collibus's small mouth. Strange picture, but it will work. For Dianne, the standard I use is "die ant." Which is exactly what would happen to an ant who was standing in front of that bus. Let's hope that doesn't happen.

You might wonder if I was using examples that would be easy to associate. The answer is definitely no. If you remembered a name, the credit goes to you. What I am saying is this. These six steps will work as long as you allow yourself to *make* them work. As far as the easy or natural associations go, if you get one, take advantage of it. Just be sure to make the association as illogical as you can in order to make it more memorable.

Take These Techniques to Heart

Review your examples as often as necessary to feel comfortable with them. Meanwhile, I would like to give you some good practice techniques for becoming proficient in this challenging and crucial area of networking. Use the following practice techniques, and the method you have learned will work like a charm.

First the Face...

For the next week, I am going to ask you to note and exaggerate the outstanding facial feature of everyone you encounter. Don't worry about remembering their names. Simply observe and exaggerate their outstanding facial features.

Do this whether they are people you are seeing for the first time or have known most of your life; whether they are business associates or members of a group, club, or organization that you belong to. And of course, this also goes for pictures in newspapers and magazines.

Get accustomed to noticing an outstanding facial feature in everyone. At first it may seem difficult. Sometimes it may take a while. So what? They will never know what you are doing. Besides, you aren't yet trying to remember their names.

Take as long as you need to isolate and exaggerate the feature. You will pick up speed very quickly. Remember the standard shift theory. It won't take long.

Then the Name

Also during this first week, at your convenience, familiarize yourself with the 1000 sound-alikes at the end of the book. After seeing the mental pictures for the sound-alikes several times, you will feel more comfortable with them.

At that point, begin glancing through your telephone book to check out the different names and attempt to make up sound-alikes for those that do not present pictures. After you feel more comfortable, try this with people you meet, while you are meeting them. Meanwhile, keep practicing with pictures in newspapers and magazines.

Slowly Bring It All Together

Here's my suggestion: For the following week, make a conscious effort to meet and remember the name and face of just one new person every day. One new person. While you are doing that, you can also do another exercise that will greatly help you to get used to that standard-shift challenge we all have while learning a new skill.

Look through a *USA Today* newspaper, take a pair of scissors and literally cut out 10 to 20 pictures of people you do not know. Without yet looking at the names, fold them under the picture. Now, one by one, slowly at first, go through the six steps to remembering each person's name. After every few, review them quickly and then go on until you have done them all. You know it will get easier and faster as time goes on.

Back to real live people. Once you have mastered being able to remember one new person's name per day, go on to two, then three, then four, and so on. Don't expect to bat a thousand—no one does. Eventually, however, your percentage will be much higher than it is now, and you'll be recognized and rewarded for that skill. Don't put undue pressure on yourself right from the start.

Enhance Your Networking

All right, so we are a bit farther on down the road. You are now ready to walk into that party, gathering, or chamber of commerce function and delight people by meeting them and then remembering their names. Can't you picture it happening? It will. Just follow these instructions.

When you arrive, walk over to someone and introduce yourself. Lock in that person's name. Then go on to the next person and do the same thing. Now do that with another person and you have met three people and you remember them. At this point, make sure you remember them by glancing back and reviewing their names.

Yes, nothing wrong with that. They will not know what you are doing. Proceed to the next two or three people, then look back and review everyone you have met up to this point. Probably five or six, right? Now continue meeting people one at a time, pausing after every few to run a quick review of those you've met.

Use your own judgment. You won't have to review every person every time, but when you get a chance, do it. One friendly warning I might give you is not to try memorizing too large a group your first time out of the gate. Begin with 5 or 6. Next time 10 or 15. After that 15 or 20.

Following that, dare to be spectacular! Actually, however many people you happen to feel comfortable trying to memorize is just fine. After doing this exercise many times, you will master the skills.

Now, make sure you discreetly show off your newly acquired ability. For example, one of the first people you met at the networking function was Charlene Foster. Forty-five minutes later you walk past her at the hors d'oeuvres table. Glance at her and say, "Hi, Ms. Foster, are you enjoying yourself?" She (being like most, unskilled in these techniques and having forgotten *your* name) will most likely be quite impressed. Do this with a few more people, and the word about you will get around: you're the one who remembers everybody's name.

Two Final Quick Points

I would like to answer a couple of questions you may have. The first is, "What if I am introduced to several people at the same time?" The answer is try to avoid that type of situation as often as possible. If there are two people, you can just try to concentrate that much harder, but it can be tough.

Any more than two or three people at one introduction, and I simply make a point of concentrating on their outstanding facial features. As the group begins to disperse, I then approach each of the people individually and inform them that, "The names were said much too quickly for me to observe them all, but I like to make it a point to remember people's names. May I please ask for yours again?" Just doing that earns you a point in that person's book for class, professionalism, and likability. And those three qualities spell both social and professional success!

After that individual person tells you her name, lock it right in, and then *remember* it. That ensures your success. Incidentally, if your goal at a function you are attending is to meet and remember as many people as possible, try to be the first person there. That way, you will get to meet a core group of individual early arrivers, which will give you an extra edge.

The second question is, "How long will I keep in my mind these strange associations for the people I am meeting?" You will only see these bizarre images or pictures for as long as you need them. After the second or third time you meet a new person, their name will become part of your true memory, and the unusual associations will no longer be needed.

Go out and do it! And make it fun!

Key Points

- There are six key steps to remembering peoples' names and faces.
  1. Observe the person's outstanding facial feature.
  2. Exaggerate the person's outstanding facial feature.
  3. Observe the person's name.
  4. Repeat the person's name (in order to ensure you heard it correctly).
  5. Form a mental picture of what the name suggests or a sound-alike.
  6. Form a ridiculous association between the mental picture of what the name suggests or a sound-alike and the outstanding facial feature.
- Make practicing fun and effective by
  1. Concentrating only on finding an outstanding facial feature
  2. Concentrating only on the name (mental picture or sound-alike)
  3. Remembering one new person per day—then two, then three
  4. Practicing on people in newspapers, magazines, and so on

14
Networking: Begin Now

It is one of the most beautiful compensations
of life that no one can sincerely try to help
another without helping him or herself.
RALPH WALDO EMERSON

Isn't the above statement a great summation of what we've been discussing throughout this entire book? Regardless of whether it's working a crowd or networking in a one-on-one situation, positioning yourself through the media, asking questions, having better follow-up than anybody else, providing excellent customer service, running your own organized networking group, or just helping others succeed in their businesses, the more you do for the benefit of others, the more successful you will be.

What never stops fascinating me is the fact that the people who give the most of themselves to others, without expecting anything in return, seem to get back many times over what they give out. And truly successful networkers do the little things right consistently, knowing that they will eventually reap the harvest from the seeds they have planted. But there's one more thing to keep in mind, as well.

This brings us to the final point. Throughout this book you've been exposed to techniques that can and will account for a dramatic increase in both your personal happiness and financial earnings, but only if you take the information and apply it!

How often has it been noted that knowledge without action is the same as having no knowledge at all? To succeed in your quest for endless referrals, you must take the information you have learned and absolutely begin applying it to your life right now!

Unfortunately, many people read a book such as this as though it were a novel, skimming through, finding some ideas interesting, maybe even saying to themselves, "One of these days I'm going to use that technique," but they never actually get around to it. I call these people "as soon as" people.

You know the type: really nice, well-intentioned people. Unfortunately, they are always in the process of "getting ready." They're "going to" do something based on future, unrelated events that one day may take place. For example, "I'm going to learn the 10 open-ended, feel-good questions `as soon as' the kids start the school year." Or "I'll develop a benefit statement `as soon as' the next sales contest starts." (That would be a great time, wouldn't it? After all, it wouldn't make sense to start now, so that the benefit statement is internalized *before* the contest begins!) Unfortunately, all too often, that attitude is directly reflected in the size of their paycheck.

I can't stress enough how important it is to jump-start your newfound knowledge into action *now*. Go back to the beginning and read this book through again and again. See, feel, and hear yourself picking up new ideas each time through, while strengthening and internalizing others at the same time.

Skip around to different chapters, seeking information for particular projects and needs. Study and internalize the various questions, methods, techniques, and skills. Do you want to focus on cross-promotion? Then sink yourself into Chapter 11. Looking to position yourself as an expert through the various media? Turn to Chapter 9. Need a review of how to work a crowd? There's Chapter 3. How about boning up on remembering the names and faces of those people in that crowd? Please see Chapter 13.

I'm so excited for you. Based on the amount of calls and letters I receive from my seminar attendees all over North America, as well as those who own my cassette tapes, I know that people are applying this system with incredible success. You can do it too! Will the payoff be immediate? Maybe, maybe not. Will you do everything perfectly the first time out? Probably not. I'm still learning how to do it perfectly. (When that day actually arrives, I'll *really* begin to worry.)

The point is this: Begin! Begin right away! Also, the ability to stick with it is a key point. If you get knocked down, get back up. If you get knocked down again, get back up again. Among my favorite self-motivators is a poem authored by a very successful man. I'm sure you've heard it before. It's entitled, "Persistence," and it reads as follows:

Persistence

Nothing in the world can take the place of persistence.

Talent will not.

Nothing is more common than unsuccessful people with talent.

Genius will not.

Unrewarded genius is almost a proverb.

Education will not.

The world is full of educated derelicts.

The slogan "Press on" has solved and always will solve the problems
of the human race.

CALVIN COOLIDGE, 30TH PRESIDENT

My suggestion is to be persistent. Do the little things right, do them
consistently, and realize that selling, networking, and life itself is simply a numbers game. Of course, when following proven techniques,
the numbers seem to get a lot better.

Learn the techniques, implement them beginning now, and be persistent, and you will network your everyday contacts into sales.

Appendix **A**

Standards

Prefixes

D'	(Golf) tee
Di	Tee
De	Tee
Mc	My, Mack (truck)
Mac	My, Mack (truck)
O'	Cheerio
San	Sand

Suffixes

Stein	Cup
Man	Man
Son	Sun
Ly	Leak
La	(Music)
Y	Eel
Ski	Ski
Quist	Kissed
Law	Nightstick hitting
Lin	Line (line of)
To	Toe

Witz   Brains
Gar   Cigar
Ton   Weigh a ton
O   Cheerio

Directions

North   Compass
South   Mouth
East   Yeast
West   Vest, pest

Colors

Black   Shoe polish
Brown   Brownie
Green   Golf green
Gray   Ben Gay
White   Whiteout

Generic

Stew   (Beef) stew
Will   Document
Williams Yams
Watt   Light bulb
Jones   Stones
Smith   (Blacksmith's) hammer
Gordon   Garden
Cohen   (Ice cream) cone
James   Games
Johnson   Yawn (from the) sun
Roy   Soy (sauce)
Burg   (Ice) berg
Art   Paint brush

First Names

Alan	Allen (wrench)
Andrew	Ant rules (ruler)
Anthony	A toe knee
Bernie	Burn knee
Bill	Pill, dollar bill
Brad	Brat
Bruce	Juice
Carl	Cow
Charles	Jowels
Chris	Crisco, crisp
Clete	Baseball cleats
Darren	Tearin'
Daryl	Towel
Dave	Save
Dennis	Menace, dentist
Don	Pawn
Doug	Duck, dug
Ed	Egg
Frank	Frankfurter
Fred	Fret
George	Gorge
Harold	Hair old
Howard	How art?
James	Games

Jeff	Chef
John	Yawn
Ken	Can
Larry	Law (nightstick)
Leonard	Lean hard
Mark	Mark, (Magic) Marker
Michael	Microphone
Neil	Nail
Norman	Normal
Patrick	Pet trick
Paul	Ball
Phil	Fill, Phillips (screwdriver)
Ray	Ray gun
Richard	Dollars
Robert	Robber
Ron	Run
Roy	Soy (sauce)
Sam	Wham
Scott	Cot
Steven	Step on
Ted	Teddy bear
Terry	Terry (cloth)
Tim	Tin
Tom	Thumb
Vincent	Win cent
Walter	Wall tear
Alice	Allen (wrench)
Ann	Ant
Barbara	Bra
Betty	Bet tees
Beverly	Bufferin
Bonnie	Bonnet
Carmen	Carmel
Carol	Barrel
Cathy	Cat
Cheryl	Cherry
Chris	Crisco, crisp
Cindy	Sin tee

Colleen	Call lean
Denise	Knees
Diane	Die ant
Doris	Lavoris
Dorothy	Dot
Eileen	I lean
Ethel	Gasoline
Gwendolyn	Dwindlin'
Hazel	Hazelnut
Helen	Hell
Isabelle	Is a bell
Jane	Pain
Jean	Jeans
Jennifer	Gin and fur
Joan	Groan
Joanne	Chowin'
Joyce	Joy
Judy	Juice
Julie	Jewel
Karen	Carrying, caring
Kerry	Carry
Laura	Law (nightstick)
Linda	Line
Lisa	Pizza
Margaret	Mark it
Marsha	Marshmallow
Mary	Marry
Maureen	More rain
Melissa	I'll miss her
Nancy	Antsy (nervous)
Pam	Bam
Patti	Pat
Peggy	Peck, pecking
Phyllis	Fill us
Sandi	Sandy
Susan	Sand
Tanya	Tan ya' (you)
Terri	Terry (cloth)

Last Names

Abbatantuono	A bat on toe, no
Abbott	A boot
Abbruzese	I bruise easy
Abernathy	A bear nasty
Abrahamson	Ape ham sun
Abramowitz	Ape ram a witz (brains)
Abrams	Ape rams
Ackerman	Actor man
Adamchak	Atom jack, atom check
Adams	Atoms, a dam
Adler	Add law (nightstick hitting)
Aguillo	A wheel low
Ahearn	I learn
Aiello	Eye (in) Jello
Albert	Prince Albert in a can
Aldridge	All ridge, old ridge
Alexander	Axel land her, axel
Alfaro	All far o
Algozzini	All go see me
Allen	Allen (wrench), all in
Allessi	All I see
Almonte	All mount tee
Alpern	All burn

Alvarez	All for S (asp)
Amato	Tomato
Anderson	Ant ate son
Andrews	Ant rules (ruler)
Anthony	A toe knee
Argenio	Our jean's an o
Arruda	A root
Artley	(paint brush) leaks
Arvidson	R (hour) fits some
Ascot	S (asp) caught
Ashburn	Ash burn
Ashley	Ash leak
Askew	Ask ewe
Asperas	Asparagus, "Oh spare us!"
Attenasio	A tin I see o
Bacher	Back her
Bachman	Back man
Badash	Bad ash
Bailey	White bottle (the liqueur)
Bain	Pain
Baldwin	Bald win
Bannon	Pan in
Baranowski	Bear on a ski
Barclay	Bar clay
Barnett	Pen net
Barrett	Parrot
Barry	Berry
Bartlett	Pears
Barton	Bar tin
Baskin	Basking
Battelene	Bottle lean
Baxter	Bags stir
Baynes	Pain
Bazarnik	Bizarre nick
Beasley	Beastly
Beck	Peck

Beckley	Peck leak
Befumo	Perfume o
Begany	Beg a knee
Belvin	Bell fin
Belzer	Bells are
Bemmish	Blemish
Benaim	Pen name
Bennett	Pen net
Benoit	Pen hoit (hurt)
Berchtold	Birch (tree) told
Berrisano	Berries sand o
Bertino	Bird in o
Bertram	Bird ran, ram
Berustrom	Berries storm
Bierman	Beer man
Bigelow	Big or low
Blackiston	Black (shoe polish) a stone
Blaine	Plane
Blaisdell	Blaze a trail
Blake	Brake, lake
Blanchard	Branch yard
Blatt	Splatt
Blythe	Plight
Bochner	Block in there
Bock	Block
Bolden	Bolting, bolt in
Bonacci	Bone itchy
Boshar	Bow share
Bostick	Boss stick
Bourassa	Boraxo
Bowman	Bow man
Boyd	Bird
Boyles	Boils
Brablec	Grab lick
Brady	Braids
Branson	Brand some
Bray	Pray

Brennan	Pen in
Brent	Dent
Brexell	Brakes (Elf)
Brice	Price
Brill	Brillo pad
Brindell	Pin (in a) dell
Britehart	Bite heart
Brophy	Trophy
Bruner	Prune, prune her
Bryan	Iron
Bryant	Iron
Buckley	Buckle
Bullard	Bull yard
Burgnon	Iceberg on
Burke	Iceberg
Buswell	Bus well, buzz well
Buttrick	(Cigarette) butt trick
Calderon	Colt her on
Caldwell	Called well
Calero	Color o
Callahan	Call a hand
Calter	Colt tear
Cameron	Camera on
Caminiti	Cam (engine) on a tree
Campbell	Soup
Cantero	Can't tear o
Cantrell	Can't trail
Caraway	Carry away
Carey	Carry
Carlile	Car isle
Carmody	Car muddy
Carnes	Cars
Carras	Carries
Carrington	Carry a ton
Carroll	Barrel
Carter	Car tear

Cassidy	Cast city
Cassin	Cast in
Castagna	Cast on ya'
Castenbotter	Cast in water
Castiglione	Castle alone
Castillo	Cast till o
Casto	Cast o
Cavanaugh	Half a knot
Cecil	Seesaw
Cerutti	Sear (burn) a tee
Chadwick	Chat candle (wick)
Chamblee	Jam bee
Chandler	Channel
Chaney	Chain E (eel)
Chapman	Chapstick man
Chaput	Shape it, stay put
Chernaault	Turn old
Chesler	Chiseler
Chilton	Chill ton
Chonko	Chunk o
Chouinard	Shoe in yard
Christopher	Cross (Christ) of fur
Christopherson	Cross of fur from sun
Christopolus	Cross of Poles
Clancy	Chancy
Clark	Park
Claus	Claws
Clegg	Keg
Clifford	Cliff fort
Cloer	Lower
Cloutier	Cloudier
Cody	Coat tee
Cohen	(Ice cream) cone
Coletrain	Train carrying coal
Colletti	Call a tee
Collibus	Call a bus
Collier	Collar

Collins	Call n's (ants)
Conant	Cone ant
Connely	Corn will leave
Connor	Corner
Conover	Can of fur
Cooper	Chicken coop
Copeland	Coke land
Corbett	Corvette
Coren	(Apple) core in
Cornelio	Corn nail an o
Cortese	Cord lease
Coverdale	Cover tail
Coviello	Cove in Jello
Crawford	Claw ford
Creedon	Cretin
Crenshaw	Can of chaw (tobacco)
Cromwell	Crumb well
Cronk	Conk
Crosby	Cross bee
Crystalowicz	Crystal O' witz (brains)
Cullen	Color in
Culotta	S' (it's) a lotta
Culpepper	Coal pepper
Culver	Cover
Cunningham	Cutting ham
Curced	Curse an O' (Cheerio)
Curran	Car run
Curtis	Curt S (asp)
Cusimano	Cuss a mean o
Dale	Tail
Dalessio	Tail is an o
Dalloway	Fall away
Dalton	Doll ton
Danforth	Den forth
Daniels	Tan L's (elves)
Dannatt	Tan it

Dante	Dent a (ape)
Danzinger	Dance injure
Darman	Tar man
Darsch	Harsh
Darvin	Tar fin
Davenport	Dove in port
Davidoff	(Star of) David (falling) off
Davis	Save us
Dawson	Doors on
De Fluri	(Golf) tee flurry, floor E (eel)
Dean	Lean
Degress	Tee in grass
Degruccio	Tee grouchy o
Deguzman	Tee cuss man
Dektor	Doctor, deck fore
Del Gaizo	Dell gaze on o
Delaney	(Golf) tee lane E (eel)
Dembski	Dumb ski
Denton	Dent in
Dershimer	Dish em' more
Desantis	(Golf) tee sand
Desmond	Dice mound
Desnoyer	Deny her
Devaney	(Golf) tee is vaney
Delvin	Devil in
Di Atillio	(Golf) tee tilling o
Di Bello	Tee bell o
Diefenback	Deaf in back
Digby	Dig bee
Dinzik	Tin sick
Dodson	Dots sun
Doetzier	Dots her
Dole	Pineapple
Donato	Donut toe
Donelan	Funnel in
Donovan	Run a van
Dooley	Dueling

Doran	Door ran
Dougherty	Dirty
Douglas	Dug glass
Doyle	Boil
Dozier	Bulldozer
Drachenberg	Drag a berg (ice)
Drysdale	Dry tail
Dubinsky	Two pins ski
Duffin	Stuffin'
Duffy	Tuffy
Dulski	Dull ski
Duncan	Dunk can, dunk in
Dunlap	Done lap (finished a lap)
Dunzik	Done (being) sick
Durant	Door ran
Dutton	Button
Duvall	Dew fall
Dwyer	Dryer
Ebersole	Ever sold
Eble	Able
Eckerdt	Egg hurt
Eckler	Heckler
Edberg	Egg (ice)berg
Edelin	Eat a line
Edmondson	Egg mound sun
Edwards	Egg warts
Egusquiza	A goose keys ya
Eide	Hide
Eikel	I kill
Elias	He lies
Elliott	'Ell e's odd
Ellrich	L (elf) rich
Elmquist	Elm kissed
Emley	M (M&M) leak
Engle	Angle
Erno	Urn o

Espinet	S (asp) pin net
Esposito	S (asp) pole sit o
Estes	S (asp) (golf) tees
Etterly	Et' (ate) a leaf
Evans	Even
Everitt	Half of it
Faber	Paper
Fagan	Fakin', ray gun
Falasco	Flask o
Farnoff	Far off
Farolino	Far a lean o
Farrell	Barrel
Faubus	Foe bus
Faucher	Pouch her
Fay	Hay
Fazenbaker	Fuzz n' baker
Fealey	Fig leaf
Fedderson	Fed the sun
Federico	Fed a reek (ing) o
Feldman	Felt man (man made of felt)
Felton	Felt ton (ton made of felt)
Fenton	Dent in
Ferguson	Fur cuss sun
Fernandez	Firm hand is
Ferrier	Furrier
Fetter	Fed her
Fichtner	Fit her
Fiedor	Feed a door
Finney	Penny
Finnigan	Win again
Firth	First
Fitzgerald	Fits a cherry
Fitzsimmons	Fits wins one
Fixel	Fix L (elf)
Flah	Blah
Flanigan	Flame again

Flannery	Flattery
Fletcher	Letch
Floyd	Flight
Flynn	Flint
Fogleman	Vocal man
Fogt	Vote
Foley	Folly
Foltz	Folds
Foran	Forehand
Fortini	Fort teeny
Forzano	Force an o
Foster	Force tear
Fowler	Flower
Frager	Faker
Frankel	Frank (hot dog) L (elf)
Franks	Hot dogs
Frasca	Fresca
Frazier	Razor
Frechette	Fresh et' (ate)
Friedhopfer	Freed hopper
Friedlander	Freed land
Gailbraith	Call breath
Galeta	Call it at
Gallagher	Call a fur
Gallahan	Call a hand
Gampolo	Game of polo
Garcia	(C)igar see ya'
Garrison	Carry the sun
Garrity	Carrot key
Garrott	Carrot
Gartner	Garter
Gaultney	Cold knee
Gelman	Kill man
Gennett	Can it
Gentin	Bent in
Gerber	Baby food

Giagregorio	Gin in cracked cargo
Gibson	(Vodka) Gibson
Gilbert	Kill bird
Gillis	Kill us
Gingras	Gin grass
Ginocchio	Pinocchio
Girten	Hurtin'
Giscard	Discard
Giuliano	Jewel in an o
Glick	Click
Golinski	Coal on ski
Gomez	Go mess, combs
Gonzales	Gone (to get) salve
Goodner	Good in there
Gordon	Garden
Gorenkoff	(Apple) core in cough
Gorgens	Gorge n's (ants)
Gorman	(Apple) core man
Gosiminski	Go see mints ski
Goulet	Goo lay
Gove	Glove, dove
Grabler	Grab law
Grabowski	Grab a ski
Grady	Grading
Graham	Cracker
Granato	Cram a toe
Gravett	Grab it
Gregory	Keg or key
Grigsby	Grabs bee
Grogan	Grow gun
Grover	Grow fur
Guerrero	Career o
Guinn	Win
Gulliver	Gull (made) of fur
Gunther	Gun tear
Gustafson	Cuss the sun
Guthrie	Cut tree

Haferkamp	Half a camp
Hagen	Hackin'
Haggerty	Hack a tee
Haley	Comet
Halloran	Hollering
Hamilton	Ham a ton
Hamlin	Ham line (line of ham)
Hamner	Hammer
Hamzik	Ham sick
Hanley	Hand leak
Hannah	Hand her
Hannifan	Hand a fan
Hanson	Handsome
Harackiewicz	Hairy carrots
Hardesty	Hard as (a cup of) tea
Harnagel	Hard bagel
Harper	Harp
Harrington	Herring ton
Harris	Hairless
Hartigan	Heart again
Hartley	Heart leak (ly)
Hartnett	Hard net
Hawes	Horse
Healey	Healing
Hebrank	He brake
Hedberg	Head (ice) berg
Heffler	Half law
Heinz	Ketchup
Heiser	Hi sore
Helms	Helm
Henderson	Hand her some
Hendricks	Hen tricks
Hennessey	Hens see
Hernandez	Firm hand is
Herron	Blue heron
Hersberger	Hurts a berger
Hersch	Candy bar

Herschfield	Field of candy bars
Hettinger	Head injure
Hicks	Sticks
Hignite	Ignite
Hilderbrandt	Hills of bran
Hiltz	Hills
Hines	Ketchup
Hintz	Hints
Hoaglan	Hoagie (sandwich) on land
Hobbs	Hops
Hodge	Dodge
Hoffman	Huff man
Hogan	Hoe gun
Holcomb	Whole comb
Hollis	Holes
Holmes	Homes
Holt	Hold
Holtzwasser	Holes, holds water
Holway	Hallway
Holzberg	Holes in (ice)berg
Holzshu	Hold shoe, whole shoe
Honeycutt	Honey cut
Hoover	Vacuum cleaner
Hosmer	Hot smear
Howell	Howl, how will?
Hugel	Ewe kill
Hughes	Use
Hurley	Hurling
Hutchinson	Huts in sun
Hyatt	Buy it
Iacovello	Yak a bell (cheeri) o
Ian	E (eel) in
Ingerbritzon	Ink her bit some
Inman	In man
Irwin	Fir win
Israel	Star of David

Issacs	Eye is sick
Jackson	Jacks in
Jacobs	J (bluejay) cups
Jacobus	Jack a bus
Jaffe	Chafing
Jagowicz	Jacks or witz
Jankalow	Yank it low
Jarrett	Jar it
Jarski	Jar ski
Jarvic	Jar fit
Jasin	Chasin'
Jeeter	Cheater
Jensen	Jam some
Jerome	Chair roam
Jessop	Chess up
Jordan	Garden of jars
Joseph	Aspirin (St. Joseph's)
Kahlert	Alert
Kahn	Snobby can
Kairella	Cruller donuts
Kaiser	Roll
Kakish	Cactus
Kallett	Ballet
Kantor	Can tore, cantor
Kaplan	Cap land
Kardis	Card is
Karlin	Car line
Keating	Cheating
Keegan	Key in
Keelor	Key law
Keller	Killer
Kelly	Kill E (eel)
Kemper	Camper
Kennedy	Can of tees (D's)
Kenyon	Canyon

Keoski	Key or ski
Kerner	Burner
Kerr	Fur
Kessler	Kiss her
Kileen	Clean
Kilpatrick	Kill that trick
Kinchen	Kitchen
Kinsey	Can see
Kippenberger	Kept a burger
Kirk	Hurt
Kirkpatrick	Hurt that trick
Kliban	Climb pin
Klimas	Climb S (asp)
Knackstedt	Nap step
Koenig	Cone nick
Kilodny	Clot knee
Kosloff	Gauze off
Kosloski	Gauze lost key
Kosovsky	Gauze off ski
Kotecki	Coat tacky
Kottich	Coat itch
Kovacs	Go back
Kramer	Creamer
Kreer	Career
Kricth	Itch
Kuhn	(Rac)coon
Kurlander	Curl land her
Kushnirak	Cushion sack
Lally	Lolly(pop)
Lamonica	Harmonica
Lange	Lank
Larson	Lost sun
Laskin	Less skin
Laughran	Laugh ran
Laventhol	Lather all
Lawrence	Law (nightstick) rents (house)

Lazaroff	Laser (gun) off
Lederman	Letter man
Lee	Leak
Leighton	Lay ton
Lenson	Lend some
Leone	Lean on me
Leonhardt	Lean hard
Lerham	Fur ham
Lester	Less tear
Levine	Ravine
Levitt	Leave it
Levy	Jeans
Lewis	Loose
Lieberman	Leaf a man
Liedtke	Lead key
Lindsay	Lindseed
Lindstrom	Lint strum
Lippet	Lip it
Lo Brutto	Low brute
Logan	Low gun
Loomis	Loom
Lopez	Low fez
Loring	Law (nightstick) ink
Losyk	Low sick
Lubinski	Lube in ski
Lucas	Look kiss
Ludwig	Lead wig
Lundberg	Lunge (ice) berg
Lutz	Klutz
Lybrand	Lie brand
MacGowan	My cow in
MacMurray	My hurry
Macaluso	Mack (truck) a loose o
Macchiarella	Match a real
Madden	Mad den
Maginn	Mack (truck) in

Maguire	My wire
Magyar	Mag(azine) in yard
Mahoney	Baloney
Malandro	Mail and grow
Malconian	Mail a cone in ant
Malinowski	Mail on a ski
Malinox	Mail knock
Malone	Alone
Malooley	My loose leaf
Maltese	Malt tease, falcon
Mancuso	Man curse o
Manning	Man ink
Manniyar	Many yards
Marconi	Macaroni
Marcott	My cot
Marcus	Mark us
Marello	My real o
Marguin	Marking
Marino	Marine o
Markevich	Mark a witch
Marko	Mark o
Markowitz	Mark a brain (witz)
Martin	My tin
Maseley	Maze leak
Massey	Messy
Mathis	Mattress
Matsuda	Mat suit
Matthews	Mat use
Maurice	More rice
Mauser	Mouse
Maxwell	Coffee can
Mayer	Mayor
Mazor	Razor
McAnlis	My candles
McCabe	My cape
McCarthy	My car tee
McCarty	My car tee

McConville	My con fill
McCoy	My coy
McDonald	My Donald (duck)
McDowell	My towel
McFarland	My far land
McGarvey	My (ci)gar v (veal)
McGavin	My cabin
McGee	My key
McGill	My gill, my kill
McGuigan	My wick in
McGuirk	My quirk
McIntire	Mack (truck) in tire
McKenna	My camera
McKernan	My fur in
McMahel	My mail
McPherson	My fierce sun
Medford	Met ford
Meehan	Me hand
Meese	Mice
Meinhard	Mine hard
Melville	Mail fill
Meno	Mean o
Merwin	Fur win
Metcalf	Met calf
Michaels	Mike (microphone) kills
Middleton	Middle ton
Minton	Mitten
Mitchell	Miss hell
Monek	More neck
Monroe	One row
Montgomery	Mount of gum
Montrone	Monotone
Morales	Morals
Moran	More run
Morgan	More gun
Morris	Morse (code)
Morrison	Morse (code) sun
Morrissey	More sea

Morton	Salt
Moskal	Moss kill
Mostad	Mustard
Moyle	Boil
Mueller	Mule her
Mullins	Mole in
Mundy	Moon tea
Murphy	More peas
Murrell	Mural
Nagel	Bagel
Naismith	Neigh smith (hammer)
Nash	Gnash, mash
Navarro	No far o
Navetta	No feta (cheese)
Naylor	Tailor
Nayo	Mayo (naise)
Nedells	Needles
Neff	Enough
Nelson	Nails in
Nesbitt	Nice bit
Nesenoff	Messy off
Newton	Fig newton (cookie), new ton
Nieto	Knee a toe
Nittolo	Knit all o
Nixon	Nicks on
Nobile	No bile
Nolette	No (don't) let
Norbeck	Door peck
Norsworthy	Newsworthy
North	Compass
Norwood	No wood
Noyce	Noise
Nugent	Nugget
O'Brien	(Cheeri) o crying
O'Connor	O corner
O'Keefe	O keys

O'Neil	O nail
O'Reilley	O really?
Ogden	Ug(ly) den
Oglivie	Ogle bee
Oliver	Olive fur
Olson	Old sun
Oppenheim	Open I'm
Oprehezen	Opra hazing
Orben	Or pen
Ortis	Oar tears
Osmond	O's (on a) mound
Osterland	O's steer land
Ostrout	O's strut
Ouley	Oak leaf, leak
Owens	O wins
Paley	Pale leak
Palmer	Palm her
Passarell	Pass a bell
Patterson	Pat the sun
Pauley	Ball leak
Pearce	Pierce, pears
Peckham	Peck ham
Pegram	Peg ram
Pelletier	Pellet tear
Peppler	Pepper
Perez	Pez
Perkins	Perking
Perlmutter	Pearl mutter
Perlov	Pearl off
Petrocelli	Pat rose sell E (eel)
Phillips	Screwdriver
Pilla	Pillow
Pimentle	Pimento
Pisonero	Peas on arrow
Placek	Pay check
Plourde	Plowed

Polhemos	Pull lame o's
Pollack	Pole lack
Poncy	Bouncy
Popovich	Pop a fist
Porfidio	Pour video
Posluszny	Poles lost knee
Poulos	Poles
Powell	Towel
Pringle	Potato chips
Pritchard	Pitch hard
Prizzio	Pretty (cheery) o
Provenzano	Pro van's an o
Provost	Pro post
Pullano	Pull an o
Purtle	Turtle
Putnal	Put nail
Quairtius	Quarter us
Quattelbaum	Bottle bomb
Quigley	Wiggly
Quinlan	Win one
Quinn	Win
Quisenberry	Squeezin' berry
Radigan	Rat again
Radziwill	Rats in well
Rafferty	Laugh a tee
Ragali	Rag gully
Raguz	Spaghetti sauce
Raguzzo	Rag goo sew
Raleigh	Roll E (eel)
Rampell	Ramp bell
Randall	Ran doll
Rapkin	Napkin
Rathbun	Rash bun
Ratney	Rat knee
Raziano	Razz an o

Reardon	Rear den
Reark	Real ark
Reddecliff	Ready cliff
Redinger	Read injure
Reeves	Leaves
Reichley	Wright leak
Reinhardt	Write hard
Rejko	Let go
Relkenis	Real tennis
Resnick	Rest nick
Reynolds	Rain old, ray old, aluminum foil
Richardson	Rich (dollars) from the sun
Richter	Rick (of wood) tear, tricked her
Riggio	Itchy o
Riggs	Ricks (wood)
Riley	Wiley
Rittenhouse	Write on house
Robertson	Robber son
Roby	Robe
Rodriquez	(Fishing) Rod reeks
Rojas	Row ha!
Rollins	Roll ants (n's)
Rondeau	Run doe
Ross	Floss
Rostock	Rust stuck
Roth	Rot
Rothstein	Rot cup
Rosseau	Lasso, you sew
Rubin	Sandwich
Rutherford	Roquefort
Ryan	Iron
Ryker	Rye fur
Sabbatini	Sap is teeny
Sabinverzi	Sap in fur see
Sadovnick	Sad of nick
Sala	Salad

Samuels	Animals
Sanchez	Sand chase
Sanders	Sand
Sanderson	Sand her some
Sannicandro	Sunny can grow
Santoriello	Sand tore the Jello
Santoro	Sand tore o
Santos	Sand toes, sand toast
Santulli	Sand pulley
Sawyer	Saw
Saxon	Sax(aphone) on
Scadlock	Scat lock, bad luck
Scala	Scald a
Scalise	Scale lease
Schaeffer	Shaver
Schefter	Shift her
Scheibe	Shy bee
Schinman	Shin man
Schleicher	Like her
Schlossberg	Shlossed (drunk) berg
Schlosser	Shlosser (more drunk)
Schmidt	(Blacksmith's) hammer
Schneider	Sly door
Schoenholt	Show and hold
Schrader	Shredder
Schroeder	Wrote her
Schultz	Schlitz
Schuppert	Sherbert
Schuster	Shoe stir, shoe store
Schwab	Q-tip
Schwartz	Warts
Sculley	Skull
Sears	Burn
Sebok	Reebok (sneakers)
Selvig	Sell fig
Senkarik	Send carrot
Sepanik	Don't panic

Sercia	Search for her
Shaughnessy	Sure messy
Shaw	Chaw (chewing tobacco)
Shay	Shade
Sheehan	She hand
Shelton	Shell ton, skeleton
Sherman	Share man
Sherriton	Share a ton
Shupe	Chute, shoot
Siegel	Seagull
Silber	Silver
Simon	Dime in
Simpson	Simp(le) son
Sitron	Sit run
Skidmore	Skid more
Slade	Slate
Slifer	Slicer
Sloan	Loan, groan
Slocum	Slow comb
Smith	(Blacksmith's) hammer
Sneed	Sneeze
Snyder	Shy door
Sobotka	Sew vodka
Solomon	Salmon
Solson	Sole sun
Sommers	Summers
Sooker	Sucker
Sorvino	Sore wine (vino)
Sosa	Sews a
Spagnola	Smack no la (music)
Spector	Spec (eyeglass) tore
Spence	Coin
Squire	Wire
Starling	Star ink, darling
Staub	Stab
Steckham	Stick ham
Stephens	Step on

Stern	Strict
Stevenson	Step on sun
Stewart	(Beef) stew, paint brush (art)
Stinson	Stand sun
Stratton	Struttin', strap on
Strauss	Mouse
Stroud	Loud
Sullivan	Sell a van
Suprun	Soup run
Sutcliffe	Sat cliff
Sveen	Screen
Swanson	Swan sun
Swaroop	Swear rope
Sweeney	Sweetly
Tandon	Tandem
Tarricone	Tear a cone
Tarsches	Tar is
Tassani	Too sunny
Tate	Date
Taub	Tub
Teasley	Tease leak
Tebodo	Tea bow doe
Teft	Tough
Teitelbaum	Title bomb
Telsey	Tell see
Tenzer	Tin stir
Terrasconi	Terrace cone
Terry	Terry (cloth)
Thatcher	Catcher
Thayer	They are
Theriault	Terry (cloth) old
Thibodeau	Tip a doe
Thomas	Thumbs
Thompson	Thumbs sun
Thon	Thorn
Tinsley	Tins leak

Tirshel	Turn shell
Tobias	Toe buy us
Tobis	Toe biz
Toney	Toe knee
Topham	Top ham
Towner	Town
Townsend	Town send
Trammel	Trample
Travers	Travels
Travis	Travel
Trebowski	Trip ow ski
Trujillo	True hill o
Tuttle	Turtle
Tyler	Tie
Udell	Ewe tell
Unger	Hunger
Uschman	Hush, man!
Utley	Hut leak
Vadnais	Bad day
Vaillancourt	Fell in court
Van Vliet	Van fleet
Vanacore	Van a core (apple)
Vandenberg	Van den (ice) berg
Vaneecke	Van "eek!"
Vanhoy	Van toy
Vantrease	Van trees
Vaughan	Fawn
Veglia	Fig leaf
Venable	Fan a bull
Venzara	Fan saw her
Verhey	Fur he
Verity	Ferret tea
Vesper	Whisper
Victor	Victory
Villaescusa	We'll excuse ya'

Vincent	Win cent
Vinho	Vino (wine)
Vining	Vine ink
Vlach	Latch
Vogel	Ogle
Volz	Volts
Voss	Floss
Wagner	Waggon her
Walesky	Wall list ski
Wallace	Wall lace, lock
Walsh	Wash
Walters	Wall tears
Ward	Wart
Warner	Warn her
Warren	Worn
Washam	Wash ham
Watkins	Watt (light bulb) cans
Watson	Watts (light bulb) in
Watts	Watts (light bulbs)
Waverly	Wave
Weber	Wee bear
Webster	Web stir, dictionary
Wedderburn	Wet a burn
Weintraub	Wine a trout
Weiss	Wise, owl
Wellington	Well ink ton
Wenderoth	Went to rot
Wengatz	Win gates
Wenzel	Pencil
Werbalowsky	Wear a low ski
Whalen	Wailing
Whaley	Whale
Whitkov	White (out) cove
Whitney	White (out) knee
Whitworth	White (out) worth
Wilcox	Will (fighting) cocks

Wilhelm	Will helm
Wilkerson	Wilt the sun
Williams	Yams
Wilson	Will sun
Windslow	Winds low
Wirtz	Hurts
Wiswell	Wish well
Withrow	Will throw, row
Wodraska	Would ask her
Woolsey	Wool sea
Worthington	Worth a ton
Wycoff	Why cough?
Yamberg	Yam bird
Yarbrough	Yard pro
Yarnell	Yard nail
Yerchin	Your chin
Yoder	Yodel
Yoho	Yo-yo
Zadvinskis	Sad fin skis
Zakon	Sack on
Zaloom	Balloon
Zarkin	Parkin'
Zenda	Send her
Zimmer	Simmer
Zoeller	Seller
Zukowski	Zoo cow ski
Zullo	Too low

Resource Guide

The following titles have either been read personally by the author or recommended to him very highly. It is suggested that you begin to build or continue to build a library of books and cassette tapes in order to fill your mind with the knowledge that will lead to your personal and professional success.

Alessandra, Tony, Phil Wexler, and Rick Barrera: *Nonmanipulative Selling.* Englewood Cliffs, N.J., Prentice-Hall, 1987.

Ash, Mary Kay: *Mary Kay: The Success Story of America's Most Dynamic Businesswoman.* New York, Harper & Row, 1987.

Bander, Richard, and John Grinder: *Frogs into Princes.* Moab, UT, Real People Press, 1979.

Berne, Eric: *Transactional Analysis in Psychotherapy: A Systematic Individual and Social Psychiatry.* New York, Ballantine, 1986.

Berne, Eric: *Games People Play.* New York, Ballantine, 1985.

Blanchard, Kenneth, and Spencer Johnson: *The One-Minute Manager.* New York, Berkeley Books, 1987.

Boe, Anne, and Bettie B. Youngs: *Is Your "Net" Working?* New York, John Wiley, 1989.

Borg, Tom: *The Service Factor.* Detroit, MI, Wilcockson & Antoinette, 1991.

Brooks, Michael: *Instant Rapport.* New York, Warner Books, 1990.

Burg, Bob: *The Memory System.* Overland Park, KS, National Press, 1992.

Burros, Daniel A.: *Technotrends: How to Use Technology to Go Beyond Your Competition.* New York, HarperBusiness, 1993.

Carnegie, Dale: *How to Win Friends and Influence People.* New York, Simon & Schuster, 1982.

Cathcart, Jim: *Relationship Selling: The Key to Getting and Keeping Customers.* New York, Perigree-Putnam, 1990.

Cohen, Herb: *You Can Negotiate Anything.* New York, Bantam, 1983.

Conwell, Russell H.: *Acres of Diamonds.* Harrington Park, N.J., R. H. Sommer, 1987.

Cox, Danny, and John Hoover: *Leadership When the Heat's On.* New York, McGraw-Hill, 1992.

Erdman, Ken, and Tom Sullivan: *Network Your Way to Success*. Philadelphia, Marketers Book Shelf, 1992.

Fogg, John Milton: *The Greatest Networker In the World*. Charlottesville, VA, MLM Publishing, 1992.

Fripp, Patricia: *Get What You Want*. San Francisco, All Reasons Publishing, 1988.

Gee, Bobbie: *Winning the Image Game: A Ten-Step Master Plan for Achieving Power, Prestige and Profit*. Berkeley, CA, PageMill Press, 1991.

Girard, Joe, and Stanley H. Brown: *How to Sell Anything to Anybody*. New York, Warner Books, 1986.

Gross, T. Scott: *Positively Outrageous Service: New and Easy Ways to Win Customers for Life*. New York, MasterMedia, 1991.

Guiducci, Joan: *Power Calling: A Fresh Approach to Cold Calls and Prospecting*. Mill Valley, CA, Tonino, 1992.

Harris, Amy Bjork, and Thomas A. Harris: *Staying OK*. New York, Avon, 1986.

Harris, Thomas A.: *I'm OK–You're OK*. New York, Avon, 1976.

Henderson, Robyn: *Networking for $uccess*. New South Wales, Australia, Murray, Child & Co. Pty, Ltd., 1992.

Hennig, James F.: *The Familiar Stranger*. Milwaukee, WI, International Management Publication, 1990.

Hill, Napoleon: *Think and Grow Rich*. New York, Fawcett Publications, 1987.

Hill, Rick: *The Fishing Trip*. Tucson, AZ, Pinnacle Publishing, 1993.

Hopkins, Tom: *How to Master the Art of Selling*. New York, Warner Books, 1988.

James, Larry: *The First Book of Life $kill: Ten Ways to Maximize Your Personal and Professional Potential!* Tulsa, OK, Career Assurance Press, 1992.

Kennedy, Dan S.: *The Ultimate Information Entrepreneur*. Phoenix, AZ, Empire Communications, 1990.

Kennedy, Danielle: *Selling the Danielle Kennedy Way*. Englewood Cliffs, N.J., Prentice-Hall, 1991.

Koltnow, Emily, and Lynne S. Dumas: *Congratulations! You've Been Fired: Sound Advice for Women Who've Been Terminated, Pink-Slipped, Downsized or Otherwise Unemployed*. New York, Fawcett, 1990.

Kordis, Paul, and Dudley Lynch: *Strategy of the Dolphin*. New York, Morrow, 1989.

Lant, Jeffrey: *How to Make a Whole Lot More Than $1,000,000 Writing, Commissioning, Publishing and Selling 'How-To' Information*. Cambridge, MA, JLA Publications, 1990.

LeBoeuf, Michael: *GMP: The Greatest Management Principle in the World*. New York, Berkeley Books, 1989.

LeBoeuf, Michael: *How to Win Customers and Keep Them for Life*. New York, Berkeley Books, 1989.

Lewis, Herschell Gordon: *Direct Mail Copy that Sells!* Englewood Cliffs, N.J., Prentice-Hall, 1986.

Lipnack, Jessica, and Jeffrey Stamps: *The Networking Book*. New York, Viking Penguin, 1988.

Lontos, Pam: *Don't Tell Me It's Impossible Until After I've Already Done It*. New York, William Morrow, 1986.

Lorayne, Harry, and Jerry Lucas: *The Memory Book.* New York, Dorset Press, 1989.

Mackay, Harvey B.: *Swim with the Sharks without Being Eaten Alive.* New York, Ivy Books, 1988.

Mackay, Harvey B.: *Beware the Naked Man Who Offers You His Shirt.* New York, Ivy Books, 1991.

Mackay, Harvey B.: *The Harvey Mackay Rolodex Network Builder.* Secaucus, N.J., Taylor Publishing, 1991.

Mackay, Harvey B.: *Sharkproof.* New York, HarperCollins, 1993.

Maltz, Maxwell: *PsychoCybernetics.* North Hollywood, CA, Wilshire Books, 1973.

Mandino, Og: *The Greatest Salesman in the World.* New York, Bantam, 1988.

Mays, Carl: *A Strategy for Winning: Winning in Business, in Sports, in Family, in Life.* Gatlinburg, TN, Lincoln-Bradley, 1991.

Misner, Ivan R.: *The World's Best-Known Marketing Secret: Building Your Business Through Word of Mouth.* Claremont, CA, Paradigm Publishing, 1993.

Naisbitt, John: *Megatrends.* New York, Warner Books, 1988.

Peale, Norman Vincent: *The Power of Positive Thinking.* New York, Ballantine, 1991.

Pennington, Randy, and Marc Bockmon: *On My Honor, I Will: How One Simple Oath Can Lead You to Success in Business.* New York, Warner Books, 1992.

Perez, Rosita: *The Music Is You.* Granville, OH, Trudy Knox, 1985.

Phillips, Donald T.: *Lincoln on Leadership—Executive Strategies for Tough Times.* New York, Warner Books, 1992.

Popcorn, Faith: *The Popcorn Report: Faith Popcorn on the Future of Your Company, Your World, Your Life.* New York, Doubleday, 1991.

Ries, Al, and Jack Trout: *Positioning: The Battle for Your Mind.* New York, Warner Books, 1987.

RoAne, Susan: *How to Work a Room: A Guide to Successfully Managing the Mingling.* New York, Warner Books, 1989.

Robbins, Anthony: *Personal Power.* New York, Fawcett, 1987.

Robbins, Anthony: *Awaken the Giant Within.* New York, Simon & Schuster, 1992.

Sanborn, Mark: *TeamBuilt: Making Teamwork Work.* New York, Master Media, 1992.

Schuller, Robert H.: *Tough Times Never Last But Tough People Do!* New York, Bantam, 1983.

Schwartz, David: *The Magic of Thinking Big.* New York, Simon & Schuster, 1987.

Sewell, Carl, and Paul B. Brown: *Customers for Life.* New York, Pocket Books, 1991.

Shafer, Ross: *How To Get Famous.*Woodland Hills, CA, Shafer Productions, 1992.

Slutsky, Jeff, and Marc Slutsky: *How to Get Clients.* New York, Warner Books, 1992.

Tannen, Deborah: *You Just Don't Understand.* New York, William Morrow, 1990.

Vilas, Sandy, and Donna Vilas: *Power Networking: Fifty-Five Secrets to Success and Self-Promotion.* Austin, TX, MountainHarbour Publications, 1991.

Waitley, Denis: *The Psychology of Winning.* New York, Berkeley Books, 1984.

Waitley, Denis: *Seeds of Greatness: The Ten Best Kept Secrets of Total Success.* Tarrytown, N.Y., Fleming H. Revell, 1988.

Walters, Dottie, and Lilly Walters: *Speak and Grow Rich.* Englewood Cliffs, N.J., Prentice-Hall, 1989.

Walther, George: *Phone Power.* New York, Berkeley Books, 1987.

Walther, George: *Power Talking: 50 Ways to Say What You Mean and Get What You Want.* New York, Berkeley Books, 1991.

Wexler, Phillip S., W. A. Adams, and Emil Bohn: *The Quest for Service Quality: RX's for Achieving Excellence.* Sandy, UT, Maxcomm Associates, 1992.

Yoho, David Alan: *The Art and Science of Personal Influence.* Bethesda, MD, Professional Educators Group, 1993.

Ziglar, Zig: *See You at the Top.* Gretna, LA, Pelican, 1984.

Ziglar, Zig: *Secrets of Closing the Sale.* New York, Berkeley Books, 1987.

Index

About the Author

Bob Burg, president of Burg Communications, Inc., based in Jupiter, Florida, is a professional speaker and consultant on the topic of business networking. A former television news anchor, salesperson, and sales manager, he is a much sought after keynote speaker and seminar leader for major corporations and associations throughout North America.

BOB BURG LIVE

As a speaker, Bob conducts seminars and training programs for corporations and associations internationally. Combining humor with hard-hitting bullet points of information, his programs offer attendees immediately applicable, real-world information that they can use to increase their (and your organization's) bottom line.

Bob also has a line of audio and video programs based on this book, which can be used for individual use and/or company in-house training.

If you'd like information on having Bob speak at your convention or meeting, or ordering his audio and video products, please call or write:

Burg Communications
P.O. Box 7002
Jupiter, FL   33468-7002
(407)575-2114 or 1-800-726-3667